D0211571

Praise for
THE RULE

Larry Hite was one of the pioneers of trend-following trading. He founded Mint Asset Management, which became the first billion-dollar hedge fund. I interviewed Larry for my first Market Wizard's book, not merely due to his track record, but also because I heard him speak and loved his droll sense of humor. I asked him why he would bother writing a book after all these years—certainly not for recognition or money, both of which he has in surplus. Ironically, I discovered he provides the answer in the introduction. *The Rule* is a breezy read in which Hite reflects on his life and provides his take on the lessons of trading and life—spoiler alert, they are both the same.

—**Jack Schwager,**
author of the Market Wizards series

Super traders that stand the test of time are a rare breed—Larry Hite is one of them; he's a living legend in the trading space. I love his book! It has great lessons for trading and life. It's definitely on my top list of stock market must-reads.

—**Mark Minervini,**
US Investing Champion, featured in
Stock Market Wizards and author of the #1 bestseller
Trade Like a Stock Market Wizard

Larry Hite's chapter in Schwager's first Market Wizards book was the one that most affected my trading and career. His Rules in this book on bet size, embracing loss, and dealing with psychology are so important to trading success. His comments on bet sizes directly led to my work on position sizing and contributed heavily to my favorable return-to-risk ratios. This book a must-read for every trader.

—**Tom Basso,**
founder of Trendstat Capital Management, Inc., and currently enjoying retirement at enjoytheride.world, an educational website for traders

I'm thankful that Larry Hite took the time to write such a personal and powerful book. In addition to sharing phenomenal wisdom and excellent trading principles, the book chronicles his life story, from underdog to the highest level of trading success. The principles he generously shares can improve your personal and trading life, and readers will come away from this book feeling empowered and ready to face life's challenges.

—**Steve Burns,**
NewTraderU.com

From a dyslexic, visually impaired youth to a legendary multi-millionaire Market Wizard, Larry is living proof that anyone can overcome and turnaround the greatest of life odds to achieve success in the financial markets and in life. This book is an inspiration to traders, investors, and anyone who wants to live their life to their fullest potential!

—**Adam Khoo,**
Asia's Leading Wealth and Success Coach, Professional Stock, Forex, and Options Trader

— THE —
RULE

HOW I BEAT THE ODDS
IN THE MARKETS AND IN LIFE—
AND HOW YOU CAN TOO

LARRY HITE

FOUNDER, MINT INVESTMENTS
ORIGINAL MARKET WIZARD

New York Chicago San Francisco Athens London Madrid
Mexico City Milan New Delhi Singapore Sydney Toronto

1 2 3 4 5 6 7 8 9   LWI   24 23 22 21 20 19

ISBN   978-1-260-45265-5
MHID   1-260-45265-4

e-ISBN   978-1-260-45266-2
e-MHID   1-260-45266-2

McGraw-Hill Education books are available at special quantity discounts to use as premiums and sales promotions or for use in corporate training programs. To contact a representative, please visit the Contact Us pages at www.mhprofessional.com.

For my grandchildren, so that they
will know they have choices.

And for all the young people born with
disabilities, in the hopes that their
limitations become a source of strength.

— CONTENTS —

— ACKNOWLEDGMENTS —

have many people to thank for help in creating this book, but I'm especially indebted to bestselling author and trend follower Michael Covel. He inspired me to undertake this project and then went above and beyond to provide intelligent, thoughtful, and astute insights that guided this journey from start to finish.

Thanks to Laura Schenone and Herb Schaffner, the editors who helped bring my voice and stories to life. Associate Publisher Donya Dickerson at McGraw-Hill was a patient and generous champion for this project, and a special thanks to Alison Shurtz for her copyediting skills.

I am grateful to Alex Greyserman, who arrived at my door 30 years ago as an enthusiastic young electrical engineer hoping for a career in finance and became a trusted colleague and partner, which he remains to this day. I would also like to thank Vikram Gokuldas, who began as a programmer and today is a fellow researcher and partner.

I want to thank my former colleague Harvey McGrath for his confidence and belief in my process.

My attorney, Simon Levin, was a keen reader and has given me expert legal advice for the past 30 years. I thank him and his son Michael Levin for sharing their memories and contributing to this book. I had the privilege of being Michael's mentor and I hope he enjoyed my stories as much as I enjoyed telling them.

Stanley Fink, my former business partner and one of the smartest men I have ever known, has been a great friend and someone I greatly admire.

I am lucky to count Howard Freedman as my lifelong friend, cheerleader, and keeper of memories. My completion of this book could not have been accomplished without the support and valuable contribution of my assistant Arlene Ward.

I am so grateful for my parents, George and Helen Hite, who showed me unconditional love. I am also thankful to my Aunt Bea, Uncle Hymie, and cousins Merle and Peter Kauff, who opened their home to me and gave me a vision of what might be possible.

I am blessed beyond measure to have my daughters Samantha and Tessa and my grandchildren Ellie and Syl and the memory of our beloved Sybil, who have given love and inspiration for everything I have ever done.

I thank my wife Sharon for her patience, beauty, and love and her family for all their support.

—FOREWORD—

You can't stop the waves,
but you can learn to surf.
—JON KABAT-ZINN

Back in the early 1990s I stumbled upon an under-the-radar trading strategy. There was this nonmainstream group of traders across the world employing something called trend following trading.

This was not buy and hold. This was not Warren Buffett or value investing. This was not prediction or efficient markets. And it was not Bloomberg or CNBC daily predictions.

It was all about riding *waves*. Get on a wave and take it up or down for profit. If the wave is really high, you don't care. You still get on and ride it as long as it's going up. This is not about trying to find a red light special discount.

Now there is a trick with this style of trend or "wave riding" thinking.

You only get on that rising wave as long as you know how much you can afford to lose. Why? You have no idea why the wave, any wave, is going up or down, so you must protect your downside. You must stay alive to play the next day.

And now here is where this alternative thinking, or living, gets really fun—this way of being is not just about the markets. You see it across venture capital, making films, sports (Brad Pitt in *Moneyball*), and even relationships.

Getting behind the scenes of this unique perspective has allowed me to author five books with hundreds of thousands in sales, publish a podcast with 700 episodes (eight million listens and counting), and even direct a documentary film.

Who are some of the big names acting as trend followers (whether they call it that or not) across the spectrum of achievement? Jeff Bezos (Amazon), Daniel Kahneman (Nobel Prize, prospect theory), Jason Blum (films), Daryl Morey (Houston Rockets, basketball), John W. Henry (Red Sox, baseball), Bill Gurley (venture capital), Neil Strauss (dating), and Larry Hite (trading).

I know one person from that elite group.

Larry Hite.

Larry is one of a handful of traders who are considered living legends in the trend following trading world. However, put aside trading for a moment because Larry's story in particular is for *you*—regardless of what direction you are headed in life.

Think of it this way: When you are betting your hard-earned money or time, you need to respect the *odds*. That means you want the odds on your side at all times. For example, look at the lottery. People have no chance to win. The lottery odds are always stacked against them, but they still line up to play as hope springs eternal.

Larry is famous for putting the odds on his side as a trend following trader for over three decades—the exact opposite of lottery delusions. That means he is betting big when he has a chance to win big, and he is not betting big when he is guaranteed to lose.

Yet what makes Larry a trader who has made a bloody fortune really interesting and relatable for everyday people? He is an original. He is not some cookie cutter suit from an Oliver Stone Wall Street film or the TV show *Billions*. He is a "wrong side of the tracks" guy. That's inspiring.

I first met Larry in 2005. He appeared in my documentary film. He has been featured in my books *Trend Following* and *The Little Book of Trading*. We have talked a lot over the years. I have hours and hours of interviews with Larry. In fact, in 2012 it was a no-brainer to start suggesting that he must write a book.

And finally—his book time was here. In the fall of 2018, while Larry was nearing the end of his first book journey, he visited me for an off-the-grid reunion in

Vietnam. Larry and his wife were touring Southeast Asia and they stopped in Saigon. We quickly met up at the scenic Park Hyatt Saigon.

Larry, oblivious to his surroundings, wasted no time, "Hit me. Give me the questions. Start!"

Does he really bring it like that with a teenager-like enthusiasm? Absolutely.

Now I was not planning an interview, but I could see Larry was chomping at the bit for a give-and-take chat. Pulling out my iPhone, I said, "Can I record?"

He said, "Sure."

I hypothetically placed him on an elevator with strangers who wanted to know what he does. Now if Larry says, "I've been a trend following trader" most people, 99 percent or more, won't know what the hell that means. How does he define a trend following trader to the novice or to the smart guy who's got his law degree?

Larry is simple about that definition.

He follows the crowd and goes where the money goes. He sees the market price and is willing to go long or short depending on how the price has just moved.

Larry is using Bayesian statistics to count. Each iteration builds on the prior. But what does that tell you? Does it predict anything? Yes, it predicts a little. It predicts the next price movement, and that's where a trend can form. And that movement can keep going because of the madness of crowds. People feed on themselves. You know when you see new highs on stocks? That happens because everyone sees the excitement and they want in on it too.

Do most people understand *this*? Do most people even get it when they are given the answer?

No.

And that means we all need a different mindset.

Larry realized early on that most people lose not because they are illiterate, but because they are not numerate. They can't count. Or worse, they don't count. You see, counting forces us to look in the mirror. Unfortunately, most of us like to be part of a crowd, part of a team. We need group affirmation. We need friends and family to love us and like us. Most of us can't step outside those borders. If we step out, we're alone. And alone can be a scary place.

The genius in Larry is how he relates these complex insights in fun and approachable ways. To show his unique *way*, I must share one of my favorite excerpts from one of my many conversations with Larry:

MICHAEL: If you make a bad decision and you don't know why something didn't go your way, you've got to get the hell out. Take your chips off the table and come back to play another day. That is terribly hard for most people to do.

LARRY HITE: Well, it depends on how logical they are.

MICHAEL: Your Spock-like logic (laughing). I just watched an episode of old 1968 *Star Trek* today.

Watched Leonard Nimoy. You're basically telling me . . .

LARRY: Leonard Nimoy went to my high school (laughing).

MICHAEL: You know what? I am like clairvoyant today. Did he really . . .

LARRY: Yeah, he did.

MICHAEL: We've now established today that Larry Hite's entire career is based off a connection to Spock.

LARRY: No, I didn't even know that, but I saw that (laughing). He was one of the people I went to high school with.

MICHAEL: You've got to be Spock-like to take your losses, don't you?

LARRY: No.

MICHAEL: You don't?

LARRY: No, you do that because that's what you do.

MICHAEL: If you don't do that, what happens, you go broke?

LARRY: You go broke and you get hurt. You've got to actually make friends with losses.

That exchange is why I was happy to pen this fore-word for Larry's book.

You see, the first thing for any organism, for any ani-mal, is *survival*. So cutting losses on anything gives the chance to endure. That's Spock-like logic, simple math, simple physics, or whatever you call it. You must adapt. Not surprisingly, one of Larry's heroes was Darwin because it was he who said it's not the fastest, not the strongest, not even the most intelligent who survives, it's the one who is most adaptable. You've got to *live* or it's all over.

But nice guys like Larry are often called evil speculators. They are painted as bad guys by the uninitiated and often jealous. Yet Larry is only saying, "Hold on, let me do my thing. I'm going to play by the rules, try to find an edge and stay alive." And that perspective then gets ostracized because the masses want group safety, not novel ways of thinking for themselves. Larry has always been willing to trade the masses' view of safety for his chance at a fortune.

When discussing the masses' view of safety versus Larry's way of risk taking, he shot back at me in typical Larry fashion: "I bet you, you're a multimillionaire." With that I knew Larry was seeking a reaction and looking for the unexpected that might unfold. I also know he is just a fun guy and I replied: "I have no money Larry (laughing). What was the famous line in *The Godfather Part II*? I'm a poor pensioner living in Miami, that's it! I'm moving down to Miami Beach. I am going to live next to you. We'll both live on a pension. How's that?"

Larry, laughing, countered: "Deal."

Wisecracks aside, Larry's philosophy is often misunderstood by the financial masses. For example, every year someone somewhere always declares that trend following is dead. The obligatory and ominous Bloomberg headline runs driving huge click-bait. Mainstream media take Larry's philosophy and reduce it to fear. Why? Because their bread-and-butter ad dollars come from a Wall Street that thinks and acts very differently than Larry and that's bottom-line threatening to what they are selling.

But why will trend following never really die? Why is Larry's view timeless? Larry sees those answers succinctly: *There are very few people who are not afraid of losing.*

I have already mentioned him, but you know who's also not afraid of losing? Jeff Bezos. Did you know that Bezos uses the same rule as Larry? All of those famous Amazon business inventions are Bezos' leftover winners. They are the winners who survived Amazon experimentation. Of course, we don't hear about the thousands of Amazon initiatives or experiments that failed. You see, risk taking in life is asymmetric—from markets to dating to everything in between. Big unexpected winners pay for the many failed experiments.

Not quoting Larry exactly, but you can damn well bet he would say just as Jeff Bezos, "If you're offered a seat on a rocket ship, don't ask what seat. Just get on." Come on. Admit it. That "take a seat on the rocket ship" attitude is brilliant! We all get it instantly, but we don't often act on it for our own lives.

Now fast-forward to early 2019. I looked down and saw my caller ID. It was Larry calling from 8,000 miles away. I picked up. Within seconds we were discussing this book and potential titles. At the time, many people (including me) were offering book title suggestions.

But this was the first time Larry had told me his view on his title. He immediately blurted out, "It's the rule. That's it. The title. *The Rule.*" He did not have to explain. He was alluding to David Ricardo, the legendary British political economist from the 1800s. Ricardo had a mantra, a timeless principle that Larry gets deep in his bones: "Cut short your losses, and let your profits run on."

That's *The Rule*.

That's Larry.

Michael Covel
michael@covel.com
Author, *Trend Following* and *The Complete TurtleTrader*
Host, The Trend Following Podcast
Larry Hite Audio Interviews:
www.trendfollowing.com/larry/

—INTRODUCTION—

Get in the Game

An old very religious man lived in Brighton Beach. One day, he heard that a neighbor had won a million dollars in the lottery. The old man was so furious with jealousy that he ran out onto the beach in front of families enjoying fun and sun and screamed up at the sky:

"God, I am so angry. I've been a good husband and father. I've worked hard. I go to church every Sunday. There's been a lottery for thirty years, and I've never won a penny!"

At that moment, the sky grew dark and a lightning bolt struck. An ominous voice came down from the heavens:

"Did you ever buy a ticket? You've got to buy a ticket.*"

---

* Overall, don't play the lottery. It's bad odds, but for illustration purposes it makes my point.

Life lesson number one: You've got to be in it to win it, and if you don't bet, you can't win. This is a deceptively simple lesson, yet I have seen so many smart, talented people say they want something but don't do a damn thing about it. They don't find themselves in the winner's circle, because they never got in the game. Why? Fear. I want to help more people overcome their fear so they can have a better life than what they know now. I also want my grandchildren and their generation to see that many more things are possible if you make the right bets—not only in your money life but in your love life too. Bets are just choices we make. There is so much we don't control in life or markets, but we do control our choices.

I'll tell you my most important idea: Your dreams are more important than your limitations. You can't do anything about your DNA or your family background. But you can choose goals and dreams—and then pursue them. In my case my dreams were more powerful than my limitations. And my limitations were severe. Now, of course, there were and are many people much worse off than I ever was, but I faced substantial hurdles. I tell the story of my beginnings in Chapter 1, but to give you the basics: I was born to a lower middle-class family, had a major learning disability, did poorly in school, and was nearly blind (completely blind in one eye and half-blind in the other). I was not handsome. I was not athletic. Today, I am a self-made multimillionaire. How did I do it? I made a bet on myself and won. You can absolutely do this too.

That brings me to why I wanted to share my story.

I did not do this book for the money. I didn't do it for the fame, because I've had that, and it always turns out to be a second job. I have close to a hundred million, mostly in cash or securities, so what *is* the answer to the question of why I want to share my story?

The real question is, "Who did I write this book for?" It's for the overweight girl who did not get invited to the high school prom. It's for the last guy never chosen for a baseball game. You know, that hurts a lot when you are a kid. It's for the star athlete too—because somewhere he, too, had hard things to overcome. In short, my lessons are for everyone who did not know how to win in grade school or high school or at any time in life—which means it's for all of us.

Look, when we were teenagers, most of us were not invited to the prom by the cool guy or girl or we never became the team captain. There's an old rock-and-roll song "The First Cut Is the Deepest," and when you're a teenager, that's when you get your first cuts.

Think about it: I was a skinny kid who became a fat kid, blind in the left eye and half-blind in the right eye, and that good eye was dyslexic. So whatever I did, I sucked at badly. At school and at sports and at life, this great insight bubbled up in my experience: When you trip over things, lots of things, and your friends call you

Mr. Coordination, what you do is you get up and you keep going.

THE FIRST THING YOU DO

You can't claim it if you can't name it. This is cliché of course, but for me it was literally true. When I was seven years old and an adult asked a bunch of my friends and me what we wanted to be when we grew up, my friends gave the expected answers: a teacher, a doctor, a fireman. When my turn came, I said, "I want to be rich like my uncle." I didn't even have a definition of what rich meant but the words just came out of my mouth. (It wouldn't be until many years later that I'd find a satisfactory definition in a book called *Rich Dad, Poor Dad*. The author said that if you could live off your savings for two or three years, you were rich.) At that young age, I only saw what people above me had. My parents and I lived in a three-room apartment. My cousin lived in a big house, so he was rich. I wanted that. Want is a very powerful thing. It drove me hard.

Fifteen years later, when I was finishing college, I was asked the same question and I answered it in the same way. I wanted to be rich. To me, money was spelled with an *F*. That was the thing I wanted, the thing I could imagine tasting: freedom. And that's why I've done all I've done: because I wanted freedom to do whatever I wanted to do. But I also wanted protection from failure. I couldn't do so many things others could do, so I needed to be rich to make up for my shortcomings.

When I look back on my friends and the people I grew up with, I see that most of us weren't that much different from one another. Yet most of them did not do that well financially and have all kinds of regret. I ask myself, was I that much better than them? I don't think so—not at all. I believe my success came from the fact that I set goals and had the will to pursue it. I can't emphasize enough how important it is that you establish meaningful goals. If you don't know what you really want, every tough choice that comes along can be overwhelming.

This is not to say that I didn't have fears like everyone else. I did. When I was only about twenty-seven years old, I made my first serious money (a story I tell in Chapter 3). You'd think my chief emotion would have been joy or pride, but in fact, this first success brought enormous fear. I was not only fearful of losing the money, but also fearful of the power and responsibility that came with it.

I invite you to follow along with my journey. I will share how I became a successful trader—and ultimately a happy husband, father, grandfather, and friend. My approach to life and investing is based on a philosophy that is neither technical nor requires pages of charts. Becoming wealthy and successful isn't simply about being right all the time. It's about how much you win when you are right as well as how much you lose when you are wrong. You see a lot of small-minded people make a big deal of winning. But if you don't win enough, then you didn't truly win anything except the ability to brag at cocktail parties to people who don't know.

You don't need to know quantum physics to become a multimillionaire in the markets or any other entrepreneurial venture. In fact, many financial theories invented by Wall Street were already started on the streets of Brooklyn where I grew up. I'll never forget how one Yale economist and hedge fund manager approached me in the early 1980s. "Larry, you should join us," he said. "You'll like the system we've developed." He explained this famous economics paper they had published. The paper analyzed how the cost of holding goods affected businesses. It found that holding onto inventory is a big money loser for sellers because of the sunk cost associated with unsold inventory. The paper presented a mathematical approach for figuring out the costs of not selling goods over time. Every day you didn't sell, you are in effect borrowing money.

But really, every Jewish peddler and their kids knew about the cost of unsold goods. I said to this economist, "My grandmother was a fruit peddler in Sheepshead Bay. If she didn't sell all her fruit during the day, she'd begin to mark it down because that was the cash that paid for feeding her family of seven that night." She couldn't read or write, but she could count. Most trading, investing, and entrepreneurial success is about counting and odds, and you can do that if you have the will.

Now this economist was a nice man. I thanked him but declined to join him. Still, I was grateful for the experience because he helped confirm for me what I suspected: A great deal of what you read about investing and wealth building is built on complicated stories and predictions that always crumble under scrutiny. Let me repeat: always. The truth of winning is much simpler than most people realize or have ever been taught.

My own life is proof that overcoming bad odds is doable with sound strategy. Seriously, I have never really worked a day in my life since my early thirties. How can that be true? Well, I loved what I did, and so work was not work like we all first come to understand. But also, I learned to set up unique systems so I could make money while I slept.

I have lived by my wits, and I have done that successfully despite my terrible struggles in school and college. Those struggles made me a curious skeptic unwilling to accept the conventional wisdom from the gatekeepers and bureaucracy merchants. As I will share in the first two chapters of this book, my early failures forced me to become comfortable with that failure and, more important, with loss, and this has become a foundation for my success.

My early years also taught me about human fallibility. That's why my investing approach is never based on predicting the future. (Hint: Nobody can predict the future!) I also learned there's too much unknown, too much uncertainty, to make bold narrative predictions about where the economy or markets are headed next. My approach to winning is about understanding our human fallibility and reading people's behavior so you can make smart decisions based in the facts of *now*, not in the unknown world of the distant future, and take steps to aggressively limit your risk. I am a trend follower. The power of following trends is that they are happening now. I use something called Bayesian statistics to constantly update me to the right now, which is a lot like following batting averages. In Chapter 4, I will show you the trend following approach to money and life. And if it worked for me, there is absolutely no reason it can't work for you too.

Be wary of experts with "new new things" or mysterious-sounding systems and "new" revolutionary research. Remember Bernie Madoff? He promised easy money and stole billions. And he is not the only bad guy out there. You want to make money? Don't buy the hype—ever. Watch the trends in the here and right now. When you start following slick reports filled with predictions, you're just finding out who has good copywriters. Wall Street's investing and money-managing institutions use fabulous stories to sell their expertise to you, and they will run the same scams 1,000 years from now.

You see, stories began at the dawn of human society to entertain and instruct the next generation. We are wired to learn from well-told stories. And unfortunately Wall Street preys off our basic human weakness to want stories.

But there is the reality for those of us paying close attention: Global financial markets are not best explained or traded by stories but rather by numbers (which are the only facts). Markets are the ever-shifting accumulation of cold economic interests competing for superiority within regulated legal systems. And many Wall Street stories are designed to obscure the numbers—the probabilities—behind real trends. I have a way of beating all of the stories. It's a way of knowing if markets are going up or down—and it comes down to a comparison of two statistics. Numbers are not as exciting or as sexy as stories you hear screamed across financial channels by the pretty people who never talked to me in high school, but numbers will make you wealthier if you use them in the right way, the way I will show you. Here's an example: If I tell you about a company that is reaching a one-year new high and show you the numbers on a chart, we are not going to argue about it. But if instead, I tell you that the CEO was a war hero who saved twenty-eight people, we might argue all day. Did he really save those people? How does this help me earn money? The one-year high of the company's stock price is all I want to know—the numbers. My success was built on creating very boring systematic trading that made me rich, and never left me debating whether the guy was a war hero or not—and even if you knew the answer, how in the world would that bit of trivial pursuit make you one damn dollar in the markets?

You can make a good living selling hype, but you can get rich by buying truth.

Over the course of 40 years trading the markets—many markets, but mainly the futures markets—I've even grown agnostic about what I trade (so long as it is legal). It could be pine nuts, pork bellies, coffee, sugar, stocks, or bonds. *What* you're trading doesn't matter as much as the *why* and *how*.

As you will see, my trading philosophy challenges conventional carnival barker wisdom that tells you to buy and hold stock because it always goes up. Who really believes that? You will also see how my philosophy can work for you not only in money, but also in marriage, life, business deals, and your career—whatever that career may be.

Cut your losses and stay with your winners. That is my credo for building wealth and achieving goals of all kinds. It's my *rule*. How do we know *when* to cut losses and *when* to continue riding our wins? You must know yourself. You must determine where your tolerance for risk lies. For example, how long can you tolerate declining returns from a job or relationship? How long can you tolerate a market going against you? I will show you how to find the answers.

Remember, in life, time rather than money is the most important currency, and we all have only a finite amount of time (at least until they figure out life extension). You can win money, lose money, and earn it back again. But time is something that you can never get back, so making good decisions with the odds on your side is the best way we can give ourselves more time, or said another way—freedom.

Now, many people don't like my way of thinking with odds because there is no hero or drama. There are no three acts. No hero's journey. No great story. But what if I told you that I get up in the morning, look at some numbers, and ask myself what is the simplest way for me to get what I want? Then I spend 20 minutes making trades and I am free to go about my day.

Getting what you want, I realized, is about learning how to make smart bets—key word *smart*. And making smart bets is about understanding basic probabilities. If I was going to get rich, I had to learn to trade in a way that would make a lot of money when I was right, and not lose too much when I was wrong. That's why my thinking, my system, is based on controlling my risk to the downside so that I never lose all of my chips. In fact, I decide how much I can afford to lose and arrange my approach so that I never lose more than that. In other words, you can't lose your shirt if you don't bet your shirt. I will remind you again and again to never risk more than you can afford to lose. Why? You're not trading markets, you're trading money. And it's your money. Only you control how much of your limited supply of money you are willing to lose. When you adapt this principle, you find it easier to get in the game. You remove the fear! I get goose bumps writing that because it's still so important to success, yet not understood by most.

Maybe some already think my world is not for them. Stop. I don't believe for a second you have to be an investor or trader to benefit from my journey. These ideas can help you figure out who you really are, and how to create the best odds of making the salary you want and having the career and life you want. In life, you can't often change the world when you make a decision, but you can make better choices. Those choices can and will make a better life for you and the people you care about. That's what I want to help you do.

My aspiration is to make an understanding of my journey 100 percent free of financial jargon. Yes, I use some basic financial terms you can easily look up on Investopedia. And colorful stories are my bread and butter, but I tell stories to show how the facts and trends work—I don't use them to mislead.

Part I tells the story of my childhood and teen years and how as a dyslexic blind kid who did poorly in school, I eventually found my way into a *calling*. I share my four foundational principles and how to apply them to the game of money and the game of life: (1) Get in the game, (2) don't lose all your chips, because then you can't bet, (3) know the odds, and (4) cut your losers and run with your winners. First, you need to understand who I am, why I chose the life I did, how I think, and how these principles can help you.

In Part II, I tell the story of these principles applied to the larger world. This includes the story of how my partners and I founded Mint, which became the largest hedge fund company in the world and the first to trade a billion dollars. The trading I did was based on sophisticated research and computing, but I have tried to demystify our process and show how you can use it to build wealth even if you go a different direction than me. I also share specific mechanics for the novice and principles for the advanced trader to consider as well. What's most important to me, however, are not the exact mechanics but the overall philosophy I have developed, which I believe is valuable for everyone from young to old, regardless of your country.

As I share my experiences, you will see how my early failures forced me to adjust to failure. More important, all major fortunes are built on a lot of small losses, which pave the way to big wins and success.

When I deliver talks to university students, I often discuss the seven questions they should ask themselves:

1. Who are you?
2. What is your goal?
3. What game do you want to play?
4. Where are you playing the game?
5. What is your time and opportunity horizon?
6. What's the worst possible thing that can happen?
7. What will happen if you get what you want?

This book is called *The Rule* because one of my chief goals is to share how the same trading philosophy I used to achieve success with money can also be effective in other aspects of life—from love and marriage to career decisions to how you cross the street. I hope my words inspire you to consider the odds that underlie all of those major decisions in your life—the ones you might not be thinking critically enough about right now. Because I am a trend follower, I ask you to look carefully at the trends and numbers you are following in your life. No one can know the future, but what are those trends and numbers telling you?

PART 1

SHEEPSHEAD, PORK BELLIES, AND BLACKJACK

1

Know Who You Are: How I Learned from Failure

One night in July 2012, the *Hedge Funds Review* had invited me to their first-ever awards night. It was a black-tie event, and the folks in charge told me they were going to give me an award. I had no idea what kind of award it would be. For a short period in my youth, I'd been a stand-up comic. Might it be the "first stand-up comic to become a trader" award? Something inside of me rebels against having to show up at events. Usually once I'm there I have a good time, but I tend to avoid crowded events that require wearing a tuxedo. Knowing I *have* to be someplace is a bit of a chore but in this case, I knew I needed to attend, so I grudgingly went.

It turned out to be a lovely night, warm, but not too humid. The event was held on the hotel roof surrounded by the lights of Manhattan. Drinks, dinner, talk, you know the deal. As the evening wound down, I still hadn't heard my name. Then, finally, the last award was announced. Larry Hite won the Lifetime Achievement Award as a pioneer of the hedge fund industry. Huge applause!

I thanked them for the award and summed up a big part of my life philosophy, "You never know what you're going to get for just showing up."

I still have my award; the wood-and-brass plaque is displayed in my office. It reads, "Larry Hite has dedicated the last thirty years of his life to the pursuit of robust statistical programs and systems capable of generating consistent, attractive risk/reward relationships across a broad spectrum of markets and instruments." The magazine also wrote, "Larry Hite, winner of the Lifetime Achievement Award at the Hedge Funds Review Americas Award 2012, has inspired a generation of commodity trading advisers (CTAs) and systematic hedge fund managers."

How did *that* all happen? How did I make hundreds of millions of dollars for my investors and partners? The success I've had—and I believe the success you can have—arrived because I always expected to fail big. Solution? I engineered my actions so that a failure could not kill me. Got that? Let me repeat it in case you didn't get it, because it is mission-critical important. I won because I always expected to lose.

How on earth could be that be possible? This truth, this counterintuitive idea, goes back to my roots, my childhood.

• • •

I was born in 1941 in Sheepshead Bay, Brooklyn. That's a universe away from the elite class of upper Manhattan. We lived in a neighborhood of working-class immigrants and first-generation Americans, mostly Italians and Jews. The Jews lived in the apartment buildings, and the Italians lived in the little row houses that lined the streets. (I never even met a Protestant until high school.) Our one-bedroom apartment was at the corner of Avenue V and Ocean Avenue, in a pre–World War II red brick building. I did not have a bedroom of my own until I was around eight years old and my parents finally managed to get a two-bedroom apartment upstairs in the same building. Up until then, I slept on the couch.

What was my parents' story? My dad was a small bedspread manufacturer. His parents had been immigrants and peddlers, but somehow his family had found a way to lend him money to start the company. He had a partner who ran the factory, and my father ran the marketing, design and sales. Many years later he confessed to me that he never graduated high school. He was a very sweet man, home every night right after seven o'clock. If you did something wrong, he might lose his temper and blow up, but 10 minutes later, he'd be in your room asking if you wanted a piece of cake. My mother's parents were immigrants and peddlers too. She wanted our family to move up in the world and early on told me I'd be going to college. How exactly that would ever happen, none of us knew.

I was an unremarkable kid, with no obvious abilities to distinguish me. In fact, I had profound disabilities. I did poorly at everything I tried and felt like a failure for most of my childhood. I tried my best to be mediocre because for me that was equivalent to winning the World Series (boy, that sounds pathetic as I write it). My two major problems that made me not "normal"? The first was terrible eyesight. I was born blind in one eye, and the other eye had very poor vision. My sight was so bad that when they conducted screenings at school, I could not see the *E*—the biggest letter at the top of the sight chart. My parents got me eyeglasses, but they could correct only one eye. So I was starting off half-blind.

Naturally if you can't see, you suck at sports. My cousin was a good athlete, and every time he threw the ball at me, I risked getting hit in the head. Whenever anyone threw the ball to me, I either missed or looked like something worse than clumsy. My mother was so kind and used to say nicely, "If there is a hole, Larry would fall in it."

The other major challenge of my childhood: When I looked at a page of text, the letters and words jumbled together. Reading was torture; I couldn't write well either. My father tried to teach me to sound out words phonetically, but I just couldn't get it. I failed at school and failed some more and failed even more. I was extremely depressed for most of my childhood. At times I thought of suicide.

Not until many years later would I learn my problem had a name. This happened long after I was out of college when I was dating a schoolteacher who was studying for a degree in special education. One afternoon, I went to her school to meet her, and while I was waiting I picked up a book from a side table, opened to a random page, and began to read. Maybe the page wasn't so random because it was the first page in a chapter on dyslexia. The sense of recognition was so powerful that I was overcome with emotion. I just cried and cried—not something I normally do. Here was the explanation for my lifetime of failing. Here was what no one could understand about me. All that childhood anger and shame came flooding back to me. I thought I'd pretty much gotten past it by then, but in some ways you never get past a start like mine.

When I was a child, no one in my world had ever heard of dyslexia, and most people just assumed I was dumb or lazy. All through my childhood the person who worried about me the most was my mother. And the more I struggled with academic work, the more depressed she became. She'd go next door to her friend Mrs. Goldberg's house and cry. "What is going to happen to Larry? He can't do anything. What's going to happen to him? How's he going to make a living?"

My father didn't worry. He informed me that he expected one way or another I would find a way to support him and my mother in their retirement years. That responsibility weighed on me hard. It left me feeling very depressed.

Jewish men of my generation were expected to do this.

Looking back, my Aunt Beattie and her family had a great influence on me. Beattie and her husband, Hymie, were the rich relatives living about 20 blocks away in a better neighborhood. Mom and Aunt Bea saw my cousin and I were the same age and put us together. I spent many weekends at Aunt Beattie's house, and it was wonderful for me. Aunt Beattie treated me well, and I noticed that their family had a different culture. Go get what you want. Think big. Their values seeped into my mind.

The truth is I had a lot of things going for me, but I couldn't see this at the time. Failure helped me be creative. I loved pretending and loved imagining possibilities, so I learned how to poker-face bluff my way through much of my early life. As many young children do, especially children with the odds going against them, I used my imagination as a survival tactic on the playground. For example, a kid might ask, "Hey, Larry, did you see that?" Whether he was pointing at a plane in the sky or something that was happening down the street, I just nodded my head automatically. Of course, I was faking it. Usually I hadn't seen anything, but I didn't want to be the kid who failed at something every other kid could do, which was seeing.

My disabilities also led me to discover that I had an active imagination and could use it effectively (probably a coping mechanism). Once, for example, during a current events class, everyone had to bring in something from the newspaper to discuss. Since I didn't read well, I hadn't done the assignment. As I nervously waited for the teacher to call on me, I happened to notice the kid sitting in front of me was drawing an airplane. When my turn came, I told the teacher that I'd forgotten the news article at home but offered to summarize what I remembered. She said yes, so I told that class that I'd read an article about a new invention, a new kind of plane that could go 500 miles an hour. The story was completely fabricated, of course, but three other kids said they, too, had read that same article. Naturally, I didn't let on. It was the beginning of my acting career. I was evidently quite convincing. The experience made a great impression on me. I thought it was really interesting that I'd just made up a fact and the other students bought it. The teacher bought it, too. People were profiting off of my imagination. I didn't know it yet, but I'd found my calling—wide open to possibilities whenever they might arrive.

Ultimately, imagination became a guiding force in my life and saved me from a darker depression that could have me wanting to end my life. Imagination enabled me to cope as a kid, but more important, it allowed me to see possibilities that others didn't see—and now I mean intellectual vision, not just eyesight.

But it was when I started high school that I had a major turning point. My grades were so hopeless that the administration considered switching me into a trade school because as far as they could see, I wasn't headed to college. First, they wanted to have me assessed by an outside education expert who worked for the New York State Regents Exams. I visited him at his office, and this nice, young man gave me some written tests. As usual, I did poorly, but he must have seen something in me because he suddenly shifted gears and said, "Let's try this another way." He gave me an oral test instead, with multiple-choice questions, even in math. I had long ago figured out how to count and do math in my head (my practice to this day). We weren't in a classroom, so the pressure was off. After we finished, he reviewed the data for a few minutes, then called my mother in.

"Larry's mathematical scores are rather extraordinary. His abstract mathematical reasoning aptitude is as high as you can get."

My mother was thrilled, of course, that her intuition was right. We went in immediately to visit Mr. Shapiro, the principal of the high school. My mom had been advocating for me to get more academic attention in the wake of my poor grades. "Here are the scores," she showed him in his office. "As you can see, he's very smart."

Mr. Shapiro glanced at the test sheets, then pushed back his chair to add more room between himself and us. "Mrs. Hite, sometimes you can lead a horse to water," he said, "but you can't make him drink." He was not interested in helping. He had to manage a thousand kids at his school. He was probably trying to get to his pension in 10 years, and we were probably expecting too much of the system to really help me. I was just one kid and he wrote me off. I just figured this was the way of high school. However, knowing my scores were uniquely high gave me more confidence to finish my high school career and graduate, but that was no guarantee of success. In fact, it just opened the door to the real world—which was even messier.

In my neighborhood, a life of small-time crime was always the career choice for poor grades. The unions and mob intermingled in that time and place, which sort of left me thinking everyone was a *wiseguy*. My father had to pay off the unions to avoid a strike at his factory, and he saw that as a normal part of business and life. I knew of lots of guys who hung out on their corner, trying to act and look tough. I dabbled in minor crimes, such as "borrowing" the car from my parents when I was only 15 or so and taking it for a joy ride, then returning it near where I'd found it. I got in a few fights and took a few punches. But early on, I knew I wasn't cut out for a life of crime. If I had to run from the cops, I'd be in big trouble because whenever I ran, I tended to run into walls.

Yet I continued to maneuver my way through high school with the feeling that *something* was driving me. Finding ways of getting around obstacles or going right through obstacles created sparks for me. When I figured out that one student collected the attendance list that went to the teachers and another kid collected the version that went to the board of education, my brain lit up as I envisioned the possibilities. From then on, anytime I wanted to cut school and go to the poolroom (where, naturally, I was not a good pool player), I intercepted those lists to mark myself absent for the teachers, but present for the board of education. I was quite proud of this achievement.

I graduated only because of the New York State Regents Exams. These multiple-choice standardized tests gave me academic survival. For example, early in my high school career I was flunking biology and the teacher informed me that if I didn't get a perfect score on the Regents, I would flunk the class. The prospect of repeating biology was unbearable, so I got my hands on test prep books and sample tests from prior years and spent a day writing out questions and answers on index cards. My plan worked. I got a hundred percent correct on the Regents and passed biology. The administrators and teachers were baffled that I could do so well on standardized tests but have such failure at the rest of my academics.

I, too, found this curious, so I studied the factors in how I managed to ace this test. For one thing, I had the power of want. I profoundly wanted to not fail biology, and this gave me the fuel I needed to study and learn with alternative means, in spite of my learning disabilities. Clearly having the questions from prior years had also been critical. Why? Because once you understand the moves of the game, you can understand how to play the game. But also, the standardized tests were multiple choice, and every question involved probability. There are five possible answers for each question, and usually two were absurd. Once you see this, you can reduce your odds from one in five to one in three. That's much better odds if we are guessing. Add to that my preparation, and I'd improved my chances even further. Managing the odds was how I passed all my Regents tests and got through high school. It's how I trade and live my life today.

Luckily I did have a few friends, and I did have a gift for making people laugh, but I was too shy to use it until my senior year. I remember the moment clearly when a group of us went to hang out at a friend's house. She lived in a very rich section of town, in an actual house with a basketball hoop in her driveway. As I was standing there, I made some quips and noticed the other kids were laughing. Suddenly, I was on a roll, making jokes and telling stories, one after the next, and everyone was listening. I knew I had the crowd, because when I was silent, they were silent. They were spellbound. What a revelation. I'd been holding a basketball the whole time we'd been talking. Suddenly I threw it backward over my head. The ball dropped into the net with a swish. It was a miracle. Everyone was shocked, but no one more than me. Now I was learning that even with my limits, there were ways I could succeed. There were ways I could connect. You see, we can all find confidence somewhere in something. But we have to get in the game of life and keep trying.

Very Short List:

My High School Accomplishments
- Graduated, eventually
- Avoided joining the local mob

I shocked my high school classmates once again some 57 years later, when I returned to the scene of my crimes at James Madison High School. Our alma mater, located in the Flatbush section of Brooklyn, has long been famed for its nationally prominent alumni, including Supreme Court Justice Ruth Bader Ginsberg, singer-songwriter Carol King, actor Martin Landau, Senator Chuck Schumer, and presidential candidate

Senator Bernie Sanders (who was in my grade though I didn't know him). Madison High School honors these illustrious alumni in a large glass case called the Wall of Distinction. I never would have imagined seeing myself there, but my lifelong friend Howard Freedman believed I belonged, so he sent them a stack of articles about my investment successes and philanthropy along with a note recommending me. I owe this honor to him. It was quite a moment. I am sure my mom would have had a good laugh (and maybe a cry too) at me, Larry Hite, being added in a ceremony to the Wall of Distinction in 2016 for my philanthropy work as well as my success as a trader. When my classmate Arnie heard of this development, he was incredulous.

"Larry Hite? Are you kidding me? He used to walk into walls!"

• • •

KNOW YOUR FLAWS AND GET COMFORTABLE WITH FAILURE

Why am I bragging about my failures? Because failure became my advantage and made me a great trader, and it can do the same for you. Let me repeat that: Failure was my advantage.

People don't want to accept their own fallibility. But when you have failed as much as I did, you understand—and come to accept—that sometimes you are going to strike out. This way of thinking will open a whole new world for you in trading and life. Failing is just one action, one discrete action. I was used to it and that made it easy for me to move on to the next action as quickly as possible. I don't care who you are or what you do; you can improve your performance by knowing you are fallible and learning to live with it. I failed so often and so badly that I learned to get comfortable with it as a variable.

Think of dating. Barbara Bush said she married the first boy she ever kissed; well in that way she was very lucky. Most people have to kiss a lot of frogs before they find their prince or princess and get married. It's just the way life is. You don't give up on love because you've had a few bad dates. We must fail at love before we find success. Love is not a game of perfection—it's one of odds.

You do have to have a certain kind of nerve to be a serious trader or bettor of any kind. You have to look at the numbers and know that you are making a bet. By definition, a bet means that it may not work out in your favor. Bets are decisions made in conditions of uncertainty. Even if you have odds of 100 to 1 going for you, there's still that chance of 1 percent against you. I dealt thousands of blackjack hands just to test this out, and what I learned is this: Once you understand your potential for failure—that is, there are times you can't win—you know when to fold your cards and move on to the next. You will do this more quickly than others who stay in the game too long, hanging on and hoping that their losing bet will turn around.

This led me to define a good bet as when you can make multiples of what you're risking, and a bad bet when you are losing more than what you can possibly make.

So many self-help plans teach you to try to change yourself. But I think you should work with what you've got. You were dealt a hand—good or bad. Play the cards you were dealt. Learn your flaws and embrace them, because that's who you are. You can change the color of your hair. You might wear tinted lenses to change your eye color, but you won't change who you are or your DNA. I just ask you to know who you are. Anyone who is honest can spend an hour on what his or her real flaws are. Be that person.

Another benefit of failure is that you learn what didn't work. Just because you fail doesn't mean that a particular action will never work, but it didn't work this time. If you find out why, then you are two steps ahead for the next game or next hand or next event.

I love this example of my way of thinking in action: As a single mother battling depression, J. K. Rowling struggled to write her first Harry Potter novel at night while her children slept. It took six years of work and many rejections before she finally got the book deal that set her on her path to becoming one of the bestselling authors of all time. She delivered the following in a commencement address to the 2008 graduating class of Harvard University:

So why do I talk about the benefits of failure? Simply because failure meant a stripping away of the inessential. I stopped pretending to myself that I was anything other than what I was and began to direct all my energy into finishing the only work that mattered to me. Had I really succeeded at anything else, I might never have found the determination to succeed in the one arena I believed I truly belonged. I was set free.

Not long after this speech, I gave a similarly themed speech to a much less successful class of students, not the winners who'd graduated from an Ivy League school, but the less lucky kids who attended special education classes at the Edward R. Murrow High School in the Midwood section of Brooklyn. Here are some of the truths I shared with them:

There were times when I was a kid that I thought about suicide. I had no one who knew what I was going through. You think you're a dummy. But you're not a dummy. But what you are going through is a lot like hell.

People tend to give up on you. In my case it was very hard to read books because I couldn't see well and I had dyslexia. But what I had was imagination . . . You don't need to see if you have imagination. It's just you on the inside.

I had to think for myself, because otherwise they were going to throw me in the garbage can. I knew that if I was going to survive, I had to take chances that weren't going to kill me. I knew I had to think, but I couldn't do it with a pen and paper, so I taught myself to train my mind.

You can train your mind. You've got to have a goal, because goals make life simple. And making life simple is the key to winning.

Part of training the mind was developing an "assumption of wrongness" not only in my trading but in every possible life decision. Developing your own assumptions of wrongness and the needed mental muscles to evaluate the probability of wrongness will give you a far greater chance of getting the big decisions right ("rightness"). Look, you are a human being, and humans are error-prone. I can't tell you how many times I've watched people with mega IQs mess up their lives because they were so used to getting As that they couldn't see or even imagine they were wrong. I was not hindered by an elite education, not indoctrinated with the notion to expect perfection, so I could see early on in life that even at the finest American schools, they don't teach you how to make the most important decisions of your life: the ones where there is no easy right or wrong answer. The schools fail us kids because we don't learn anything about odds there. That's pretty amazing, right?

KNOW WHAT YOU NEED AND KNOW WHAT YOU WANT

Once you know yourself, you know what you can do, what you have done, what you are capable of, and where you can fall short. But that's just the start. Next, you need to know what you want. I can't emphasize enough how important it is to know what you want and set a goal for the next one month, one year, and your life. That's because what you get depends on what you aim for. If you ain't aiming, you ain't getting. And I needed to succeed—that was my aim—success. Need is an enormously powerful force, because from your needs you establish desires and goals. Assess what you need and be 100 percent honest with yourself, and then decide what you want as big as you can imagine.

Successful people know what they want and share a passion for goals. I tell young people to write down their goals. But it's important for all of us. Make a list of 5 or 10 goals for your life, then put it in the drawer and come back to it in a couple of weeks. Refine it. Narrow it. Then rank your priorities. Now you are starting to see how my system works.

But come on, this is not easy. It's human nature to avoid setting goals because goals force us to reconcile conflicting desires. Developing goals and writing them down forces us to stop watching Netflix or playing with the newest iPhone. You need to persevere in the process

I describe or you will fail. My goal of becoming rich was for a number of years in conflict with my goal of sleeping till noon and not wearing a suit and tie to work. And yes, I almost forgot: not having to show up for work at all, if I didn't want to. Ultimately, understanding the degree to which my goals conflicted provided a means for reconciling them, as you will see across my story.

Once you set your goals, ask yourself if you have the desire and need to achieve them. If so, you are lucky; it will make life much simpler for you than it is for others. Having a beacon-like clear goal means you can make choices based on what you really want in the long term. You will know with each choice whether you are closer to your goal or further from it. Find your desire and wants. Focus on them as if your life depended on it—because it actually does.

When I found investing, I knew I'd found my life's work. Why? Investing offered a path to wealth, and remember, my goal was to be rich. But also, investing is challenging, you meet interesting people, and the markets don't care where you came from, whether you have a learning disability or bad eyesight, whether you are black, white, Jewish, thin, fat, gay, or straight. The market doesn't judge you. Said a little more like we might have said on the Brooklyn street corner? The market doesn't give a damn about you. But in return, and this is a golden truth, you can get rich and owe the market nothing. I love investing because it is about the truth and I found a place where I could be myself. And it's turned out OK. I wanted to be rich and I became rich. But I also have had a good life and a lot of fun along the way. If you train your mind, you can too. Maybe with my logic you make a billion dollars (not great odds there) or make only a million dollars (much better odds there), but my insights, my hard-earned lessons, are where we all start.

2

Find the Game You Love: My Education as a Trader

As a young man, I didn't know how I would support myself, my future family, or my parents who were expecting me to take care of them in old age. (I later told my father this was an extremely bad bet based on what he knew at the time.) When I graduated high school, there was absolutely no reason for me to go to college. In fact, there was a substantial body of evidence against me going to college, as it seemed clear I wouldn't do much there, but my parents (mother) had drilled it into my head, so I tried. I started at a small school and soon decided it was not for me. I returned to New York City and took some courses, first at Pace University and then at The New School, but nothing seemed to stick. I just couldn't see an upside to it. Yet I kept trying for my parents' sake.

In the Column of No Regrets

There was a time when George Lincoln Rockwell, head of the American Nazi party, was doing a rally in New York City. I thought to myself: I wasn't going to let this guy talk about killing Jews in my city. I was 19 or 20 years old at the time.

I organized a bunch of my friends who had been in the army and marines. We went to the event and walked into a nearby grocery store. I said to the owner of the store, "How much to buy all the tomatoes in the store?"

He looked befuddled as he eyed me and my tough-looking friends. Probably no one had ever asked to buy all his tomatoes before. He said his price, and I agreed.

By now, a big crowd had gathered on the street around Rockwell, who set himself up on a high platform. It seemed that more than half of the people surrounding him were Jews who had come out of anger. (New York City was not a smart place to do a Nazi rally—but maybe his point was to create outrage and get attention.) We started throwing tomatoes at him. Other people were doing the same. Rockwell kept speaking, while ducking tomatoes. We made it hard for him, and we got the message across that he wasn't welcome.

When I reached in the bag for the last tomato, someone else was reaching for it too. I looked up at this younger kid I didn't know. Later I learned he was Polish, not even Jewish, and he didn't even know why he was there, but he was fighting me for the last tomato. We tussled a bit, and a cop came and grabbed the two of us and one of my buddies and threw us into the paddy wagon in the back with all the criminals, who were mainly Jews doing the same thing, including some older guys who'd fought against Hitler in World War II. Finally we got to the station and got arraigned. Because of the Polish kid, we were sent to juvenile court, and my father's lawyer got us out.

Overall, this resistance was a small thing to do. But I remember it all fondly: throwing tomatoes at that Nazi and tussling with the young Polish kid over the last tomato. I file it under the column of No Regrets. No doubt you have a few moments such as these to conjure from your memory to bolster your courage when the time comes to make a (smart) bet in your life.

I still had my clear goal of great wealth, but I had a major handicap: I didn't want to work terribly hard, and I didn't want to do anything I didn't want to do. It was a conundrum to be sure as to how I would amass my fortune, considering I didn't want to have to show up anywhere I didn't want to be.

In the meantime, I needed cash to survive. When my friend's father—a very well-connected guy in the painters' union—offered a bunch of us an opportunity to make some money, I jumped at the chance. He explained that real estate developers were in a hurry to refinish and rent apartments in Greenwich Village and Soho before a new law passed, capping the maximum rent they could charge; any apartment rented before the deadline would be grandfathered under the old higher-rent guidelines. No wonder the rush was on. The union rep brought us to a big building where the apartments were almost ready except for one final painting step: detailing the door frames, which needed first to be stripped using steel wood to scrape the excess plaster. For each apartment we completed, the developers would pay us three bucks. I tried scraping a couple door frames and knew immediately I was going to do a terrible job.

Suddenly, I had an idea and asked my friend if we could take a ride in his car over to the Bowery. Now this was in the sixties when homeless and near-homeless men stood (or slept) in every doorway on that infamous street. I walked around asking who wanted to make a few bucks, telling them to meet me at the building in the Village. I was shocked when a few guys actually showed up. I offered them each two dollars an apartment to do the job, bought them scrapers, and showed them the basic technique. They were glad for the opportunity to work. This went on for the better part of a summer. Each guy on my crew made two bucks per doorway, and I made one dollar—a 50 percent mark-up.

By September, my friends, who had worked very hard scraping and painting in the heat, made a few hundred dollars each. I, who had not worked at all, made nearly a thousand dollars. This was my first real experience of making a significant profit with very little work. I was exhilarated. Word got around, and the local union (read, mob) guys were impressed by my skills and offered me some other projects. Once again a life of crime beckoned, but I strongly suspected that it could have a very bad ending.

Acting was my only real career interest at the time. I'd become so good at faking things when I was growing up that I'd come to enjoy the art of pretending on stage. Also, as I mentioned, I was somewhat funny. So I started going to auditions and doing stand-up comedy and improv at small clubs in Greenwich Village. Acting appealed to me because I had no other real skills. Plus, people in show business made a lot of money, right? I wanted to give it a shot, but traditional pursuits called to me.

So my struggle to complete college continued. By now, I had matriculated in the only school that would take me: the NYU School of Commerce. I had no interest in business, but the admissions officer made it clear I could take writing and acting classes so long as I took the minimum requirement of five business courses to graduate. So that's what I did. In between classes, I kept showing up at auditions, hoping for my big break. Movies were where the money was, so I wrote a couple of scripts with a partner (I could never write a whole script myself), and we even sold a couple. But the movies never got made.

Early career lessons from a trader who never went to business school:
- Profit is the residue of other people paying you for labor you didn't do.
- The key to understanding your opponent's behavior is motive.
- Where you lack cash, look for leverage.
- Pay attention to who isn't laughing when everyone else is.

When I finally got cast in a couple of bit movie parts, I had a rude awakening. It turned out that movies were rather hard and tedious. We'd shoot a scene, but then someone would discover that a klieg light had moved to the wrong place, so we'd have to shoot it all over again. Then something else would go wrong, and we'd have to do yet another take, and then another and another. It was such a pain in the ass. I'd loved the spontaneity of improv, but the movie process was not for me. And if I wasn't going to be a movie star, then why do it?

That was the end of my acting career. I cut my losses, but I took away certain winnings as well. During my time as an actor, I'd studied method acting, which was perhaps the best thing I ever learned in my life. I'm talking about the style of acting made famous by Lee Strasberg at his Actors Studio in New York City of the 1950s. Method acting encourages actors to explore the inner emotional lives of their characters. That means understanding your character's goals and how he or she would most likely set about achieving these goals. In essence, method acting teaches you to perceive other people's motivations, and I have used this technique to inform my investing and trading decisions ever since. Why? Because human nature—that is, our still-primitive lizard brains—drive financial markets. Our longings, needs, greed, fear, ambitions, and creativity build the driving forces of supply, demand, trends, booms, and busts now and throughout history and always will.

At that time, however, the most urgent question was, What would I do with myself to make big money now that my acting career was over before it started? I needed to find something else, but I didn't know what.

That "something else" took me by surprise one day in finance class when the professor—a small, neatly dressed Connecticut guy with a great sense of humor—was explaining various financial instruments. He described stocks and bonds with the usual reverence you'd expect of a business professor. Then he got to commodity futures. For the general reader who may not know, commodities are the raw agricultural products, fuels, and metals that get traded around the world and turned into food, energy, clothing, and a million other things. When you buy stock, you actually own a piece of a company. But since it's not exactly practical to buy huge barrels of oil, corn, cocoa, or sugar and store it in your garage until you want to sell it, commodities traders access these markets by buying and selling futures contracts. Basically, they trade bets on future prices. Many people then and now think this is highly risky—even if they have no clue about the details.

My professor said commodities were the craziest markets of all because you could trade on a huge amount of leverage—meaning borrowed money; sometimes you needed to put up only as little as 5 percent of the total trade in cash.

At that moment, my brain jolted awake. Had I just heard him say that with a mere $500 cash in a margin account, you could trade $10,000 in commodities? It seemed too good to be true.

Evidently, my professor didn't think so. He saw the commodities market as an absurd amount of risk. "These people trade on a 5 percent margin, and most of them borrow *even that*," he said incredulously. The whole class laughed except one person who later went out and became a multimillionaire. That was me. I thought these crazy traders seemed pretty smart. They could make huge deals with relatively cheap loans, by putting up only a small fraction of the money. What was so funny about that? Being able to bet with money that wasn't yours seemed like a brilliant idea. Plus, every day your 5 percent deposit stayed in the margin account, it sat in US Treasury bills. If Treasury bills paid 3 percent, then the real cost of my margin deposit wouldn't be 5 percent, but really 2 percent. That was very cheap money. And may I point out that this revelation was not fancy mathematics, but simply counting (remember I learned early that this was one of my skills)? Counting is something I highly recommend when you are looking to shift the odds in your favor.

It was plain to me that in commodities you didn't have to have an empire. You could be a nobody from Sheepshead Bay and borrow money at a dirt-cheap cost and pay it back one transaction to the next. It seemed smart to me.

I also realized my teacher really didn't understand the difference in the level of risk between placing your money in a single commodity versus holding a portfolio of 20. One bet going down 5 percent would happen, but all 20 bets going down 5 percent was much less likely.

I began to learn everything I could about commodity futures. Now most people believed this trading was dangerously volatile. Many years later, I would learn through my own testing and data analysis that over time, commodities are no riskier than stocks. Yet, it's true that commodities are subject to a particular type of volatility that seems to strike fear in some people. For one thing, many agricultural commodities are highly influenced by weather. A huge ice storm in late spring can ruin a season's crop and send prices suddenly up. Now add geopolitics to the mix: Since raw materials are grown and extracted all over the world, wars, violence, tariffs, transportation problems, and government subsidies can all send prices up or down. Traders make money by speculating on these price changes. If they think the price will rise, they will go long, meaning buy at a low price and sell at a higher one. If they think the price will be dropping, they will go short, which means they borrow a certain amount now and repay the commodity later, when it is lower and they can keep the difference. And of course, I repeat, the beauty of it is that you can do it on leverage.

In *Hamlet*, the character Polonius tells his son "Neither a borrower nor a lender be." Shakespeare may have been a genius, but I knew this was bad advice. Business-people should borrow. Why? Because then you *have* the money, and you can use this leverage to your advantage. Yes, I understand that the word *leverage* scares people—especially in trading, because if you were to lose your shirt, then they'd come and collect everything you owe with the dreaded two words: margin call.

But what if you could play the game as you wanted to play it and risk only what you could afford to lose? And what if you minimized your risk by making 20 small bets instead of placing everything on one or two? What were the chances of all 20 bets going down at once? Pretty small. And what if you cut your losses quickly once values started to drop, so you wouldn't risk more than you wanted? These ideas would eventually form the foundation of the investment approach that earned me millions. But at this time, I was only just beginning to figure the game out.

I had one more key insight about markets from my college years. At one time I had a business with another kid in college selling term papers. I got my hands on a couple of successful term papers and rejiggered the opening statements and conclusions and switched stuff around. Many of the students I knew took the same classes, and what I noticed was that under some teachers, one student got a high mark and another student got a low mark on what was essentially the same paper. Why did one person get a higher mark than another? I concluded that it happened when the teachers weren't reading the papers carefully, but also it was the relationship the teacher had with the kid. This gave me a jaundiced view of the "grades" marketplace. It was not an efficient market. I would soon come to know that efficient markets don't exist and never will as long as humans are playing the game with greed and fear in a tug of war. (I'll tell you more about the myth of efficient markets later on in the book.)

• • •

With my epiphany about the markets and trading, I had found my goal. I wanted to be a trader in these wild markets. But I had no idea how to get into the game. So after I graduated college (finally, after six years of trying not very hard), I found work as a music promoter to make money. I represented bands and took a share of the gate at rock clubs.

One night in 1964, I even met the Beatles' manager Brian Epstein at a rock club I was promoting in the East Village. I liked Epstein and would never forget him. We had a lot in common—he was a working-class Jewish guy who grew up with a dad who kept a store. Epstein said he had placed a bet on the Beatles because he wasn't going to go broke promoting the Beatles, a band who had already taken over the Liverpool and UK music scene, but if they broke out internationally, he had a chance to win very big. The best part: If things didn't pan out, he had a backup plan. (You always need the backup plan.) His father had a successful record store back home, and he could always go back and get a job. Of course, his bet paid off very big, but sadly it didn't last for long. He may have managed his career risks quite well, but he took way too big of a personal risk, mixing drugs and alcohol. In 1967, he was found dead of an accidental drug over-dose at age 32. His death saddened me very much. It was powerful evidence that you have to take smart risks, and taking a big risk with your life definitely isn't smart.

My rock promoter career didn't last long. One week-end, there were three separate shootings in clubs where I was managing bands and as a result one of my best musicians quit. It was a major loss, and I realized that the music business was just too much risk I could not control. It was then I decided it was high time to pur-sue my dream of getting into trading. Like I said, I had no idea how to do this, but knew I needed my foot in the door right now with all deliberate speed.

In 1968, that door opened just a crack when I got hired at Edwards & Hanley, a brokerage house. As a lowly desk clerk taking orders for stocks (I wasn't very good at it), I was the guy who took the boss's car to be washed. But eventually they promoted me to the position of broker because they thought I'd be good at sales. They were right. I sold stock and was good at it. But I didn't like this one bit. At Edwards & Hanley, these guys were just stockbrokers who'd gone to better schools and wore better shoes. That is harsh, but I saw too many pitches and calls that overstated future returns, hid bad ones, and buried simple math in mumbo-jumbo words.

How did I really know it wasn't for me? I figured that out on my first day when I used the phrase a "good bet" when talking to a client. I'll never forget my red-faced managing director who got all huffy and puffy with me.

"We don't bet at Edwards & Hanley," he said. "We are not running a casino!"

I used my acting skills to feign that I understood him. But I went home and looked into it because his explanation did not temper my skepticism. I quickly learned that the term *blue chip* comes from the Monte Carlo casino where the most expensive chips are blue. Hence the term *blue chip stocks* refers to the most expensive stocks on the market and supposedly the biggest and safest in which you can invest. This confirmed what I'd suspected all along: that the stock market game is all about gambling, and gambling is all about odds. Now that I knew my boss was wrong, the question was, "How can I put those odds in my favor and win?"

At Edwards & Hanley, I was soon making 40 or 50 thousand a year selling stock, but I didn't want to be part of this Wall Street mystique that all too often was just a smoke screen for poor results. I didn't really want to have clients or bosses. And I certainly didn't want to sell. Instead, I wanted to pour all my energy into research—learning and testing my investment ideas without having to make political decisions, influenced by people's needs and desires, which as far as I could tell were basically irrational.

I soon met a trader named Jack Boyd who was consistently making money. Back then, most commodities guys traded futures in individual markets. Traders who worked sugar didn't talk to the guys who traded wheat. Jack was the only person I knew who was trading in many different markets, which appealed to me. So I asked for a job and he said yes, offering me 20 grand a year. My father thought it was the stupidest thing he'd ever heard. But I didn't care. When you are young, you can live at home or live with a roommate; it doesn't matter, so long as you are going where you want to go, going where you *need* to go.

LOOKING AT THE ODDS

I went to work for Jack Boyd at DuPont, Glore Forgan Inc. and started a whole new learning process. He was not particularly scientific, but he had a method that interested me. When he saw something move, he went in that direction. When it didn't go in the right direction, he got out. He did not call himself a trend follower, but he did practice the cardinal rule of trend followers: Cut your losers and let your winners run. When a market started to decline in price, he got rid of it no questions asked. When something was on the rise, he bought in no questions asked. He controlled his risk by spreading his bets. He broke with the typical practice of specialization and traded across many markets. I counted up all his trades and found that he made about 20 percent a year. He had a lot of losing trades, but they were only small losses. And his winners were few, but they were big-time gains. Sometimes only one or two trades accounted for the majority of his profit that year. Lightbulb moment!

I now knew I wanted to do what Jack Boyd was doing but with far more scientific rigor. One of the things I believe most in in this world is the scientific method, that is, testing your assumptions. So I sat down at my kitchen table and laid down my charts. I wanted to test my ideas and use the results to develop mathematically proven rules for when to go into a given market and when to get out.

Because I didn't know classical mathematics, I looked for a simpler model to investigate. Eventually I found Edward O. Thorp's famous 1962 book, *Beat the Dealer*. Thorp (a mathematics professor turned trader) tested thousands of blackjack scenarios and devised a system of card counting in which anyone could use the basics of probability and increase their odds of winning. Thorp spent a year running these scenarios using a massive room-sized computer at MIT.

I couldn't run a computer or put data into it. I couldn't do the things that a dyslexic couldn't do. But I was inspired by the idea of Thorp's work with cards and probability. I'd come from a family of card players and grew up in a family where there were always decks of cards around. My mother and father used to have family and friends come over to play. Look, I may not have had access to a computer, but I had an affinity for cards and counting.

I was in my late twenties, and it was summertime. Everyone was going to the beach, but instead, I sat there like a professional chess player who plays thousands of games. All summer long, whenever I had free time, I dealt myself Las Vegas Solitaire, which is solitaire with a twist in that you turn over every card instead of every three cards. I was studying probability, and what I discovered was that under certain circumstances, you can lose. Sounds simple, I know, but bear with me. Even with the advantage of being able to look at every card (instead of every three), I could still lose. Even when I gave myself every chance to win—even bending the rules, I still could lose. That really hit home to me. I proved to myself that losing is sometimes inevitable even if you do everything right—that's because you always assume the risk of losing is there. I began to think hard about this. How could I prepare for the inevitable?

FOUR KINDS OF BETS

Most people think there are two kinds of bets: good bets and bad bets.

Through my early experiences and other research I began to see there are actually four kinds of bets: good bets, bad bets, winning bets, and losing bets. Most people would assume that if you lose it's because you made a bad bet and if you win it's because you made a good bet. But that's wrong. Good and bad bets refer to the odds. Winning and losing bets refer to the outcome. You can't completely control outcomes. But you can control two things for sure. The odds of the bet you take, and the risk you take.

Let's say there are two perfectly matched sports teams going up against one another. A friend bets you a dollar that his team will win. If you accept, the odds on this bet are fifty-fifty you will win. The potential payoff is two dollars versus a one dollar risk. That's a good bet. Why? Because you stand to make 100 percent on your money. And you can lose only a dollar. You can afford to lose a dollar, right? Can you risk 10 dollars to earn a potential 20 dollars? Perhaps, but what about a one-million-dollar bet at fifty-fifty odds? For most people, much bigger numbers make it a bad bet and not worth the risk. For Jeff Bezos, it's fine to risk a million dollars because he is worth $150 billion. This is *how* you think about bets and odds.

Now what if I put a plank across the floor and tell you I'll give you a million dollars if you walk across it? That's an unbelievably great bet. But what if I put this plank on the 50th floor between two buildings on a windy Manhattan day? Need I say any more?

If you keep placing good bets, over time the law of averages will work for you. But you must never forget you will still lose sometimes. That's just the laws of probability in an uncertain world where prediction doesn't work. If I know this in advance, I am prepared to bet only what I can afford to lose.

Be forewarned that one of the worst things that can happen is for you to get lucky on a bad bet and win big. For example, you walk across the street looking intently at your cell phone ignoring everything. That's a bad bet. You could get drilled by an old guy who can't see over the wheel. But guess what? You're lucky and you don't get flattened. In fact, you are not lucky, because this is how you become desensitized to risk. What happens next? You brazenly continue your mindless walking practice until you get hit by a bus. If you keep placing bad bets, over time the law of averages will work against you. This is essentially the probability you never learned in school condensed into a useful heuristic you can use now.

These are simple and powerful concepts you can apply to every area of life. Why? Because every day we make bets with our time and our money, our energy and our love. What are the odds that if you give your time and energy to someone, you will reap rewards of a happy productive relationship? How much time and energy can you stand to lose? At different phases in your life, the answers will change.

In the Introduction to this book, I told you to get in the game, and in the last chapter, I told you to know yourself. Now I urge you to find the game you want to play and ideally choose to do something you love because that's a good bet for success. Why? If you are having fun, you won't mind working a little harder. And if you love what you do, it isn't work. I was lucky to find my way to trading. To me, figuring out how to create things that would make me money while I slept was great fun; I enjoyed it so much I would have done it for free.

3

Working the Odds: Your Time and Opportunity Horizon

I n the mid-1970s, I had moved from Jack's firm to a commodity house, Hentz, but that didn't work out, so I decided to go out on my own. I started off by raising small funds and got several investors in the $50,000-to-$100,000 range. I did a few of these funds, and they performed extremely well, which gave me a small track record of success.

But getting to the next step was a challenge. I didn't have a big name, and I didn't have big connections, so getting big money under management was tough. Even proving I could double people's money wasn't enough. And when I mentioned the word *futures*, people would think only maniacs do that. Plus, I was betting across commodities markets, and people felt that was even riskier, no matter how well I made the case that it in fact was less risky mathematically than the stock market, because it was diversified.

I realized I needed to offer customers something to get them in the door—a kind of gimmick. One day, I happened to pick up a 12-page booklet in a local brokerage firm. It covered the tax implications of options trading. That weekend I was at Fire Island. I left my friends and sat on a dock for three hours trying to read and learn it. It took so long not only because of dyslexia but because of the way law is written—everything refers to something else. When I got through it, I understood I could create a partnership so my investors could convert ordinary income into long-term capital gains on their tax returns and save an enormous amount of money. This was back when the top income tax rates for Americans were at 70 percent. Capital gains tax rates were much, much lower. Depending on the particulars, it could be as much as a four-to-one write-off, meaning that investing one dollar in my fund allowed someone to write off four dollars of income. I also saw a way to change losses from being counted as capital losses to ordinary losses, which were better deductions. Understand all of this was totally legal. Big financial firms did it all the time.

I took this concept to my attorney Simon Levin. (Our joke is that I am a pretty good tax lawyer.) He looked into it and confirmed it was possible; then he did the legal work to make it happen. When I worked with Simon, it was one plus one equals three.

This was a major turning point for my company. Our offering was unique, and it highly incentivized investors to bring their capital to me. This did the trick. Soon we had $5 million under management and then $10 million, and other firms were trying to copy us.

In the early 1970s, pork bellies—which, by the way, is where bacon comes from—were attracting huge amounts of trading. The market had only started a decade earlier when meat-packers came up with the brilliant idea of pressing pork stomachs into massive 40,000-pound frozen slabs (bigger than some houses). Hog farming had always been volatile, but now with a standardized frozen unit, meat-packers could warehouse their product for long periods and better control their supply and protect themselves from gluts and shortages. For those younger readers who don't remember, those two words "pork bellies" were made famous in the film *Trading Places* with Eddie Murphy and Dan Aykroyd, and other places in popular culture as a catchword for how commodity markets worked.

Not long after I got started in "bellies," I noticed a trend: If you bought in the fall and sold in July, you made money. No expert I asked could explain why this was true. I started to read books and studies on meat manufacturing, and I found out that Americans consumed a lot of bacon during the summer because of the popularity of grilling and, of course, BLT sandwiches. This explained the increased demand. But I also learned that during the summer, supply dropped because more pigs perished during transport in overheated train boxcars. But remember, I don't look at the market and tell it what to do. I let the market tell me what to do. At any rate, I verified everything and got ready to execute this trade idea.

The problem was, I had very little money. So I took an OPM approach—as in other people's money. I asked people to invest. Remember that most people don't have the time or expertise to know how to invest, but if you've done your homework and have a well-thought-out idea with good odds in your favor, you can convince people to take a chance on you and get your first investment capital. So many people get their start this way, whether in the markets or launching a business. A guy asks a hundred people to help him start his first restaurant. Seventy-five say no, but twenty-five say yes. A couple of decades later, he has built restaurants from coast to coast. It wouldn't have happened if he didn't have the chutzpah to ask people for that initial investment. This is how I made my first big trade, too. I raised about $100,000 by going to family and friends and asking them to invest with me on my pork bellies trade. I put 10 percent up front myself and charged them 20 percent for performance. That meant I stood to gain 30 percent while putting up only 10 percent of the cash. My plan worked. I more than doubled our money and then some—$100,000 turned into $250,000—a huge amount at the time. Trading like this came very easily to me because I could accept being wrong. But I also loved the speed of that trade. It was like I had dropped a Mercedes engine into a Ford and I was off to the races.

• • •

However, I was shocked to discover I did not feel great happiness at making all this money. In fact, I felt great fear. All my life I'd been limited by disabilities. Now I had defied all expectations and won big. I'd have no excuses anymore for not being successful. But that was the heart of my problem. I could now feel the expectations rising both inside myself and from others. Even my girlfriend at the time started ratcheting up the pressure, telling me that now we had enough money to get married. (I didn't want to do that.) I was simply not ready for success. I suspect I was afraid of having maximum freedom. Being able to do anything can be very oppressive. Now who do you blame for your mistakes? What if you make a choice and you don't like it? Now you have to make your own happiness. Money ain't that hard, but happiness? That's a whole different story. I wasn't ready.

So naturally, I went right out and lost all that I'd won.

Next, a colleague who worked in corn commodities came to me with his plan for a big trade and tried to get me to join him. He said we couldn't miss. He knew a lot of facts about corn and seemed on top of it, so I trusted his judgment and followed him into the trade. Turned out he was wrong, and I had risked a lot more than I had.

In fact, the bet had been a good bet, in theory, but widespread rains triggered one of the biggest crops in history, which sparked a record drop in cash corn prices. A drought would have wiped out large sections of the crop.

I watched in horror while corn futures began plummeting. Minute by minute my money disappeared before my eyes. I was heavily leveraged with a huge bet, on my way to owing more money than I had. If the loss was too big, I knew I might never recover.

I was so desperate that I walked out of the office into the stairwell. Even though I'm Jewish, and Jews don't kneel, I got down on my knees and prayed: "God. Please don't give me a debt," I begged. "I don't care if I don't make money, please just get me out even." At that moment, a bunch of guys from Switzerland came down the stairs and were startled to see a young man in a frumpy suit kneeling and praying. I must have looked ridiculous.

"Sir, do you need some assistance?" one of them asked.

I stumbled to my feet. "Thank you, no." Then I went back into the office to face my fate.

Corn prices recovered enough so I did eventually break even. I have no idea how it happened. Maybe God answered, or maybe it was luck. No matter. That trade was a huge learning experience. For one thing, I took the corn guy's tip on faith without doing any of my own research. But more important, it was an enormous lesson on risk. I realized I had bet far more than I could afford to lose. I had placed my bet considering the upside (as so many people do), rather than the worst-case scenario. I vowed never to do that again. Don't forget, lesson number one is to get in the game. You can't win the lottery if you don't buy a ticket. But lesson number two is equally important: If you lose all your chips, you cannot bet.

Review

- Lesson number one: Get in the game
- Lesson number two (just as important): Don't lose all of your chips, because then you cannot bet.

FOOLS RUSH IN

After my corn debacle, I never wanted to be on my knees again. I learned the hard way that I had to respect risk. That meant arithmetic—not prayer—because it was clear to me that successful trading was all about odds. I wanted to compute those odds and then test them with various investing strategies to figure out what would beat the market. My goal was to build a model based on probability.

I was looking for angles that would put the odds of winning more in my favor. And in this way, I got interested in the emerging field of game theory, which, simply put, is the study of a strategic decision making. Game theory uses mathematical models to predict interactions among players who are operating under set rules. It presumes that all players are rational and will act in their own interests. You could say that game theory has been around in some form or another since ancient times when generals planned their battles, but the theory became formalized in 1944 when a mathematician, John von Neumann, and an economist, Oskar Morgenstern, teamed up to publish their paper "Theory of Games and Economic Behavior." Since then, academics and businesspeople have applied game theory to every possible field: philosophy, psychology, politics, auto insurance, marriage, evolutionary biology, the arms race, and yes, of course, poker, too.

In the early 1970s, I went to the NYU science library and read as many books as I could on the topic. My goal was to publish a paper that would increase my reputation and credibility. Most of the books I found were filled with advanced mathematics that might as well have been hieroglyphics as far as I was concerned. I had to rely on the prefaces, which summed up the material. Still, I understood what I wanted to say, which was that to make a good decision, you need to know where you are and what your choices are. I was not a mathematician, so I needed to find someone who could check my ideas. In fact, throughout my career I always needed quantitative people and computer experts who could execute my

50

ideas. Because I had no money at the time, I was happy to share credit or give people equity rather than pay them.

In 1972, I met Steve, a young quant who'd just graduated from Tufts. He and I copublished an article, "Game Theory Applications," in the *Commodity Journal*. It became a pretty big deal, because no one had written a proof of how game theory could be applied to trading futures, but this is what we did.

We began by quoting Albert Einstein, who wrote that his special theory of relativity had been based not on speculation, but rather on "a desire to make physical theory fit the observable facts." The key words here were "observable facts." We wanted to use this approach to determine probability. As we explained in our paper:

> We would look at a set of observable facts, or a single fact, which is followed by an event. Then we count the total number of times that those observable facts occurred, and divide by the number of times that these facts were followed by the event. That's how probabilities are done.

In other words, if you think the market will act a certain way under certain factual conditions, test it a thousand times to find out the odds.

Next, we considered that games always have a set of rules. The rules benefit somebody at some time and determine the only alternatives available. For example, once cards have been discarded, you can't go back and see which ones they were. That's the rule. You have to watch and remember them in order. Another example: Some people get to go first, second, or last, and so on. Each of these positions convey certain advantages and disadvantages. One thing people fail to understand about professional athletes is how well they know the rules and try to use them to gain advantage throughout the course of a competitive contest. And we were thinking just like pro athletes.

Then there were the possible moves. Game theory showed that you have three alternatives: call, raise, or fold. Assuming you have monitored the options, what are the odds of winning with each of those options?

The point of our paper was this: Taking into account the (1) observable facts, (2) the rules of the game, and (3) the available three options (call, raise, or fold), you get a chance to pick—without much penalty—when and if to bet. Time, is therefore, a powerful tool in your arsenal.

To show the time horizon in action: Let's say you are playing blackjack and you've got 17 in your hand. You need a 4 to win, but you've already seen two 4s come and go. So what's the chance of you getting one of the two remaining 4s? Pretty bad. Let's say you have a 1 in 20 chance. That means that it *can* happen, but it's not a good bet. Don't take it. Wait for a better bet when the odds are in your favor. This is what I mean when I say that you control the timing of your next bet. This is your advantage as a speculator.

At a casino poker table you have to put money in the pot before you see what happens. But as a speculator trading commodities futures, you don't have to do that, because you don't have to play the market at all to see what will happen. You can watch until you see the best probability of value and then choose your moment of entry. Has a stock or commodity been on the rise for the six months? Has the 30-day average of a particular commodity been reaching a threshold to prove you have a rising trend you should follow? If not, then wait. Then when it crosses your threshold, only then, you buy in and follow the trend.

> The next time you are in the throes of a decision, feeling that you need to make a bet on something, stop and ask yourself, what are the *observable facts*?

Understanding your time horizon makes for an amazing life skill. Should I marry this person? Do I buy this house? Do I take this job? Should I retire? These are all important bets. If you have leeway as to your when, then you have powerful advantage. You can time your bet for the circumstances and timing when you have the best odds of success in your favor.

• • •

BETTING FOR THE BIG WIN

So by now, I hope I've made it clear that making room for *losing* and *respecting risk* are cardinal rules. But here's something just as important. You have to always be on the lookout for bets that have a huge payoff without huge risk (we call this *asymmetrical*). Remember, if you're always winning but winning only small amounts, then you aren't really winning anything.

Here's why: Playing a small game all the time is not safe. If you have only small gains, you won't provide for the many small losses you are going to have. See, I make my money in chunks. The average person, not yet aware how the game really works, always goes for steady small money because it seems like a safe bet. The problem is that this is not as safe as it seems, because if you don't have a lot of money, you're not protected from those losses that inevitably come—whether it's a bad trade or a sudden health problem or whatever. What if you get cancer and a drug that is a guaranteed cure costs a quarter-million dollars? If you don't have that money, you did not play it safe at all.

To make big money, you have to always bet on something that has a potentially large payoff. If you do this regularly, then eventually the odds will work in your favor and you will win big over time. This is why you should always be on the lookout to bet on an ultra-powerful opportunity. These don't come along every day, but when they do, you have to be in. This is what I mean by a horizon of opportunity—a time when we have the chance to make a major win that can change everything about our life right now.

In the mid-1970s, I found one such major opportunity in the coffee market. At the time, prices were extremely low; there was a glut of supply, and farmers were getting killed. After researching 50 years of weather patterns and supply/demand data, I saw that coffee consumption had been rising for a long time, but prices hadn't yet responded. I was sure they had to, so I went and bought calls on coffee option futures, betting their value would rise. I was not focused on the size of the return but on the odds that one of the world's most beloved beverages would rebound in value.

The odds were very good, so I decided to bet one million dollars over the course of a year. I did this by buying options $250,000 at a time, which was the equivalent of what I was earning every two months at trading. This was a big bet for me at the time, but I asked myself if I was prepared to lose it. The answer was yes. I was prepared to take the loss if the trade went bad, but I had done exhaustive research about the trend that pointed in one direction. So probabilities told me my bet could net a big gain.

There are two kinds of bets: a good bet and a bad bet. A good bet is defined as having a high probability of making more money than you are risking. A bad bet is when you risk a lot for small or limited gains. As a speculator you should be in the good bet business.

At the time (early 1975), coffee was trading at 60 cents. A year later, it was up to a dollar. A year later, it was up to two dollars. Very good friends of mine would call and say, "Okay Larry, you have made enough money. You're up to $6 million. Cash it in." But I said, "No. The trend is still going up." There was a 32-year-old guy at the trading house working at the computer watching it and he couldn't handle the stress. But I rode the trend from 60 cents to $3.10 and my initial $500,000 went up to $15 million. When the trend reversed and went down I got out with $12 million. Emotionally, it was a major moment. I was 35 years old, and I had $12 million dollars. No one in my family had ever had $12 million. This was a life-changing breakthrough for me.

Yet inside of me a voice was saying, "It can't be this good." I was emotionally not ready to be a big winner. Some people love success and can never have enough. But when I got that big hit. I said to myself, I can't do that again, $500,000 to $12 million in a year? What are the odds of that happening again? Instead of working out why that worked, I said to myself, "Boy, you were lucky." There is truth to that. Philosophically speaking, I was lucky. When you talk to refugees who escape from their home country horrors, understanding the role of luck becomes very clear. If you were born in Syria and your house is bombed to shambles, it's hard to have a dream.

I recently visited Cambodia and saw the killing fields where Pol Pot slaughtered up to three million people. It makes you realize that even if you are born into a lower-middle-class American family, you already beat some amazing odds. So I figured that considering I had hit the lottery in the first place, and then made a giant leap to living in a mansion thanks to this huge coffee trade, I'd gotten as lucky as I could hope for. So I laid a little bit low for a couple of years. I bought a nice house for my family. I did my normal trading, which was very satisfactory and made me a living.

In retrospect, coffee taught me something I want my kids and grandkids to know. If you play in a big game in an intelligent way, you can make a lot. If you are in a game where you can make a lot of money, you have to accept it.

I was prepared to bet $500,000 because I was willing to lose it, and I had some idea that I could make $3 or $4 million dollars on the $500,000, but it turned out to be much more. Now it would be a while before I'd really learned to accept this, but sometimes, you get more than you thought in life.

BEATING THE ODDS OF DATING

Long before the dating books of today, the ones that teach about *odds* and *games*, I decided to apply my investment strategy to my dating. And just as with investing, you can't win if you're not in the game. The problem for me was that in dating, the first bet people take is usually based on looks. I was not good looking—that was a simple fact—and therefore a social scene of a party or bar was not a great place for me to succeed with gorgeous women. So I came up with an idea to play the game differently in a way that increased my advantage of at least getting to the first bet. First step? I went to shopping malls because that's where women strongly outnumber men. Then I kept my eye out for an attractive woman who was by herself looking a bit bored or perhaps on a lunch break. I'd go up and ask if she'd like to have a coffee. Since it was in a public place, it was safe, so this was not a ludicrous suggestion. About one in four women said yes.

Then we'd have coffee. I was sure to show an interest in them and not talk about myself—also putting odds in my favor. If we got on well, I'd take the next step and ask them out to dinner. Only one in three would say yes to dinner. If that went well, we'd start dating. Using this method, I drank a lot of coffee and dated a lot of fabulous women. If someone is having trouble dating the right people or even dating at all, putting the odds in your favor like I did will always work.

I didn't meet my wife Sybil at the mall, however. I met her on Fire Island one summer when I shared a house with friends. She was one of my roommate's guests, and the first time we met we wound up talking all night. On our first date we spent the whole evening laughing together. She thought I was funny, and she liked to laugh. Things continued to go well. We both wanted children; so we got married and had two wonderful daughters. Sybil was a very proper British woman who came from a family of socialists. Both she and her mother were social workers. She and I were very different from one another. I used to say to her that we are both in the social work business at different ends of the spectrum, "I help very rare people, the rich, while you help the people who are more common—the poor." One person gave the other a different view of the world, and we had quite a good marriage for 32 years until she passed in 2008. In the next chapter I will share more on how my approach to trading also works for love and marriage. For now, suffice it to say that I made a great bet on Sybil.

• • •

I hope you find value in the fundamental insights that go into my method. It relies on following the trend. It suits me and who I am. I don't like to stress myself. For me, trend following is simple and it works. And it has made me a lot of money.

This method is also aligned with my strengths, and soon it was easy to turn it into a positive system. The result is I have invented my own bias based on a novel method that works for me. That's why I use so many examples based on my personal experiences. Since I know what happened in my own life, all of this is verifiable—I have lived it.

A Loser's Guide to Winning

I once went to a horseracing track with a guy who was supposedly "can't miss" in playing the ponies. His father was a bigwig at Saratoga, and to keep from getting bored I started to bet too. I looked at the sheet and did nothing but spread a whole bunch of small bets across all the horses with the longest odds of winning and therefore the highest payouts. I didn't care about the individual horses (I knew nothing about them). I was indifferent to the outcome of each bet. At the end of the day—literally—I had pocketed quite a good sum of money—much more than my friend who knew a hundred times more about the horses, the racetrack, and the conditions than I did. In that case, my nearly complete lack of knowledge worked in my favor. Think of my horseracing experience as the loser's guide to winning. I spaced out the bets and made them small enough so even all together, if I lost every one, the outcome couldn't kill me. I played to *survive*.

But as I experienced success, I would sometimes ask myself *why* it happened. Many years later, I was at a table with colleagues in England after we'd all made many millions on the Mint Guaranteed Ltd. Fund I'd launched. These guys were generally of the Cambridge and Oxford ranks, and I went around the table and asked each one, "How much smarter are you than your father?" Each of them said that they weren't smarter, or not much smarter, than their fathers. I replied, "Then why did we make ten times more money than our fathers ever made?" I told them that we'd launched beyond our fathers' genes, not because of our brilliance, but because we'd placed the right bet where our risk was minimized and the upside was great. It was an issue of *technique*. It was about a *rule*. This is why when bets are placed correctly, enormous life gains are possible.

You have a choice as to whether you set your priorities and place bets to achieve them, or have your life dictated to you by events. You must use all the tools in your arsenal to put the odds in your favor. Timing is an edge; use it to place your bets strategically. And the size of your bets plays a huge role. At the outset of each major move, ask yourself, "How much can I make?" Because the payoff has to be worth it, right? And finally, "How much can I lose?" Because you don't want to bet your deli to win a pickle.

4

Trend Following: Cut Your Losses and Let Your Winners Run

B ritish-born David Ricardo (1772–1823) is one of my personal heroes and a brilliant classical economist who had a huge impact not just on me but on the world. Let me share a bit of his story and you will understand why.

Ricardo descended from a family of prominent Sephardic Jews who were expelled by the Catholic church in Portugal and settled in Holland. His Dutch-born father, Abraham, moved his family to London (where Ricardo would later be born) and became a very successful stockbroker on the London Exchange and leader of the Jewish community in London. As a teenager, the young Ricardo began working at his father's side learning the trade, but he was an independent thinker and not always on board with his father's traditional ways. At age 21, Ricardo eloped with Priscilla Ann Wilkinson, a Quaker, and the young couple became members of the Unitarian Church. He broke ties with his family and went off on his own with barely any funds. Because of his good reputation, he was able to start his own business in the markets with the support of an eminent bank house. Ricardo made his living in the markets and did really well. But his passion was the world of ideas. He studied economics and math and by his late thirties began publishing his views on free trade (he was a staunch believer) and wages, currency, labor theory, political economy, and the law of diminishing returns. Along with John Stuart Mill, Adam Smith, and Robert Malthus, he helped create modern economic theory and influenced generations to come.

In his own time, his reputation largely rested on a single bet, for which a lifetime of trading and speculating had been merely a dress rehearsal. In 1815, Riccardo bought British government bonds at rock-bottom prices, betting on the outcome of the Napoleonic Wars (legend has it that he did so with advanced knowledge, but this is unclear). When word got back from Belgium that the Duke of Wellington had beat Napoleon at Waterloo, British securities soared, and practically overnight Ricardo became one of the richest men in Europe, with a million in sterling, which would be in the region of 80 million British pounds today.

After Ricardo's death, a British newspaper editor named James Grant described the secret of Ricardo's success:

> Mr. Ricardo amassed his immense fortune by a scrupulous attention to what he called his three golden rules, the observance of which he used to press on his private friends. These were, "(1) Never refuse an option when you can get it; (2) cut short your losses and (3) Let your profits run on."
>
> By cutting short one's losses, Mr. Ricardo meant that when a member had made a purchase of stock, and prices were falling, he ought to sell it immediately.
>
> And by letting one's profits run on he meant that when a member possessed stock, and prices were rising, he ought not to sell until prices had reached their highest and were beginning again to fall.

I have now shared with you three of the cornerstones of my approach to trading and life: Get in the game. If you lose all your chips, you can't bet. Know, and improve, the odds.

But the fourth is the most important. It is Ricardo's Rule, for which I have named this book: Cut your losses, and let your winnings run. Put simply: When something is not going well, stop doing it. When something is going well, continue. This rule is at the core of my trend following approach to trading. I quote it nearly every day.

If you prefer country music, you can quote the legendary song "The Gambler": "You've got to know when to hold 'em, know when to fold 'em, . . ."

Here's how it works: To spot a rising trend, you look at where the price is now relative to where it has been. So for example, if the price of a commodity or stock is higher than it has been for 40 or 50 days, more people believe it is higher, so you can buy and ride this trend. When to get out? I simply ask myself how much can I afford to lose? If the answer is 2 percent, for example, then as soon as the price comes down by 2 percent, it is gone from my portfolio. That's how much I'm willing to risk. In other words, cut your losses quickly and stay with your winners. This is what makes you money.

STATISTICS RULE

Let me be clear: I did not invent trend following. There were trend followers before Ricardo, and trend followers after him. Richard Donchian, for example, is sometimes called the father of modern trend following. He was a trader who graduated from Yale and MIT and noticed that commodity prices often moved in trends, meaning that if something went up or down, it would likely continue in that direction for at least a little while. In the 1960s, he started writing a weekly newsletter called

Commodity Trend Time, publicizing his "four-week rule," strategy. He bought when prices reached a new four-week high and sold when they reached a new four-week low.

So it is not that trend following wasn't out there. It was. But my partners and I were among the first to automate it by creating a systematic approach based on data and using backtesting. In other words, we proved it worked using the scientific method. We also had great timing. The emergence of increasingly powerful computers during the 1970s that we could actually access made systematic research possible. In fact, a trader I know, Ed Seykota, was one of the first to create computerized trend following trading and he was using punch cards at first!

But I always say: I was driven not so much by greed as by laziness. I wanted money to work for me, not the reverse. My goal was to create a system I could put on autopilot so I didn't have to anguish myself over the ups and downs of the market. This way I could sleep at night, and even better, make money while I was sleeping. I did not do this because I was arrogant—quite the contrary. Having failed at so many things in my childhood and youth, I always presumed my own wrongness and limitations. To get around this human fallibility, I wanted instead a rigorously tested statistical approach that was proven on large numbers. I explained it this way to Jack Schwager when he interviewed me for his book *Market Wizards*:

What makes this business so fabulous is that, while you may not know what will happen tomorrow, you can have a very good idea what will happen over the long run.

The insurance business provides a perfect analogy. Take 1 sixty-year-old guy and you have absolutely no idea what the odds are that he will be alive one year later. However, if you take 100,000 sixty-year-olds, you can get an excellent estimate of how many of them will be alive one year later. We do the same thing; we let the law of large numbers work for us. In a sense, we are trading actuaries.

Trend following isn't a strategy solely for commodity markets or futures; you can use it for stock trading as well. Recently, a friend told me he was buying a major chunk of Microsoft stock, and he was doing it from a trend following point of view. We discussed how Microsoft now leads the cloud server market with overall year-to-year growth of more than 50 percent. A recent fiscal year just ended showed 100 percent growth. As of my final review of these pages in late February 2019, Microsoft is still trading near its 52-week high of 116 dollars per share. In 2018, the S&P 500 index as a whole *lost* 6.2 percent.

That is certainly a very strong trend, and there are many possible explanations for this strong performance. To name a few: Microsoft aggressively invested as the leader in enterprise cloud technology, which is now a booming business. A strong CEO has been at the helm for some years. And, the company still has its lucrative model of licensing outside partners. These factors are certainly influential and interesting. But the underlying fundamentals of a company are not what motivate me, a trend follower. A trend follower will buy Microsoft stock because the stock price is rising and has been rising long enough to establish that there is a trend in place. The trend follower will not try to predict how long it will last. When the trend falls, he or she will get out. In other words, I don't make money because I know anything. I only make money because I do what the market tells me to do. See, I prefer averages, kind of like a bookie, with my risk spread far and wide so that no single trade is too emotional. I like my workplace to be boring (screaming at a monitor was never something I wanted).

In the world of trading, some traders analyze the non-stop avalanche of market data using various software packages to make numerous trades on a day-to-day, hour-to-hour basis, exploiting micro swings in the markets and hedging losses. Some of these techniques can work if backed by the biggest banks and huge staffs. But too often traders get so caught up in their charts and never-ending data sets that they lose touch with the big-picture opportunities staring right back at them. I don't need a million charts or thousands of pieces of fundamental data to tell me that Microsoft's cloud business is booming—the trend is telling me. It's telling you too.

Look, I respect the sheer intelligence and devotion of economists and historians who have attempted to understand global markets and develop a unifying theory of human behavior and market dynamics. But I don't believe any such theory will hold up to scrutiny in the real world of money on the line.

When you start believing you have remarkable market predicting powers, you get into trouble every single time. To repeat myself, I've always built an assumption of wrongness into my trading, and this should be a mandatory practice in your own financial life too. Keep asking, "What is the worst thing that can happen in this scenario?" Then the worst-case scenario is my baseline. We always want to know what we are risking, and how much we can lose.

Interestingly, trend followers have tended to do well during times of crisis. Why? Because big sell-offs create dramatic trends across all markets. As my friend Michael Covel discusses in his book *Trend Following*:

> For markets to move in tandem, there has to be a common perception or consensus about economic conditions that drives it. When a major event occurs in the middle of such a consensus, such as the Russian debt default of August 1998, the terrorist attacks of September 11, 2001, or the corporate accounting scandals of 2002 [and the 2008 equity market crash], it will often accelerate existing trends already in

place ... events do not happen in a vacuum. ... This is the reason trend following rarely gets caught on the wrong side of an event.

With the help of modern automation, systemizing my rules, I move quickly and don't wait for the markets to drop 50 percent, and thereby lose more than I can afford to. I get out, preserve my capital, and look forward to the next rising opportunity, because there is always a next one coming.

BUT WHAT ABOUT BUY AND HOLD?

What I am describing is quite different from Wall Street's conventional advice, which tells investors to buy and hold with a passive approach to their portfolios. In this school of thought, you should do nothing when prices drop. The idea is not to pay attention to fluctuations in the market, but rather wait it out, because over time, the stock market always rises and you always do well.

This buy-and-hold approach is based on the efficient markets theory that markets are rational because everybody has access to the same information, and prices adjust accordingly to their right value. Put simply: The market always wins. Therefore, mere mortals cannot pick stocks that will do any better than the S&P average.

I've bought low and sold high in my life, and I believe, unequivocally, that when this approach succeeds, it is a happy accident. Why? Because no one can know for sure that a property or stock or whatever market or life endeavor will eventually rise and when. Yes, you might do very well with a buy-and-hold strategy. But you also may have to endure booms and busts and potentially major losses for lengthy periods—losses many people may not be able to tolerate. For example, looking at the historic S&P Index, it's clear that if you had money in an S&P Indexed fund in the early 1950s and withdrew it in the early 1970s, your buy-and-hold strategy would have worked brilliantly because the market was soaring when you exited. But what if you didn't want (or need) to take it out until April of 1982? You would have been heartbroken because the S&P had dropped again dramatically.

Never, ever forget that no one can predict the future. History is littered with successful companies that unexpectedly fell beneath the weight of time and change. I remember when Enron was the company of the future. Where did Enron wind up? No matter what anyone says, you shouldn't believe they know what will happen economically or in the markets years from now. To speculate this way is dangerous. We live in a hyper-growth high-tech entrepreneurial economy where industries rise and fall in less than a decade. The profession of setting type by hand had been around for hundreds of years, passed down for generations. Then the computer arrived and digital typesetting wiped out the profession in just a few years.

Another great example? Uber has only been here since 2009 and it is now worth about 60 billion dollars. Uber, Lyft, and Grab have crushed the taxi and limousine industry worldwide. I'll bet that before 2009 every Uber stockholder who was not from the company never thought for a minute that yellow cabs could become as outmoded as a horse and buggy.

Consider the telephone. When my older daughter was a teenager, I knew who she was going out with because the phone would ring, and we'd answer and ask who it was. Then we called her to the phone, which back then was something that came out of the wall. Three years later, I had no idea who my younger daughter was dating, because email had arrived and that's how she arranged her social life and dates. Today, if they both weren't married, they might use Tinder, which arrived in 2012 and became the instant dating software of choice for adults of all ages by eliminating the fear of rejection from meeting potential dates through its double opt-in navigation. The app's parent, Match Group, was recently valued at $3 billion (2017). When was the last time a young person called another young person and "asked them out" on a date? Tinder's swiping interface will, I am sure, spread in different forms to job searching and other areas I can't predict. And I'm sure that at some point it will be replaced by something else. We live in a throwaway society and in that kind of world . . . my *rule* is sound.

FIGURE 4.1 **Trend Following Compared to Buy and Hold**

Trend following (Societe Generale's the SG CTA Index) compared to equity markets (the S&P 500 Total Return Index) from January 2000 to June 2019.

Source: Alex Greyserman and Kathryn M. Kaminski.

I am not saying that you should not strive to buy low and sell high. Nor am I saying that the buy-and-hold approach is wrong. There is no single trading or investment approach that works every time. This is why it is best to mix and diversify. Back when we started, trend following was radical, because people thought you must use fundamental information to make market decisions. A quant method such as trend following, which just used price to buy and sell, was sacrilege. Trend following is about odds, and Wall Street is about telling stories and making predictions (people sadly pay a lot for predictions). So not surprisingly many advisors still push buy-and-hold asset investing to the exclusion of other approaches, but it is now possible to diversify because today there are mutual funds and exchange traded funds (EFTs) that allow ordinary people to gain exposure to trend following approaches that complement their traditional portfolios.

In a study that compared average annual growth, my colleague Alex Greyserman and his coauthor Kathryn Kaminski found that during this 20-year period between 1992 and 2013, trend following outperformed (as measured by the Barclay CTA Index) equities (as measured by the S&P Total Return Index). Most revealing is that if you had combined both approaches equally, you would have done best of all.

	Barclay CTA Index (at equity volatility)	S&P Total Return Index	50:50 Combination
Average Annual Return	10.9%	9.22%	10.37%

Source: *Trend Following with Managed Futures: The Search for Crisis Alpha* by Alex Greyserman and Kathryn M. Kaminski.

TREND FOLLOWING FOR LIFE

The Austrian School economist Ludwig von Mises (1881–1973) wrote that "one must never forget that every action is embedded in the flux of time and therefore involves a speculation."

I agree. Life is a constant series of bets that we must make every day in the face of uncertainty. In life, as in the markets, we are wise to admit what we do not know. We can use only the observable facts at hand as we make decisions, knowing that we can be wrong.

Humans are not rational in markets or life. For example, we all know that to lose weight we should just eat less and move more. So why don't people do it? I like to use love and dating as examples when I try to help people understand my ideas. Far more people are experienced with the quest for love than they are with the quest for a fortune. We all can relate to the power of attraction, the pursuit, and the joy of finding a partner, as well as the disappointments of losing at love. After all, we humans are, above all, wired to procreate, which is why the drive to pursue romantic partners is very strong.

There is something quite comparable in money and love, and that is risk. When we give ourselves to someone, it is a big risk in exchange for a big gain—or so we hope. Usually we do not stay in a relationship unless we are receiving something positive. How long do we stick with a bad trend early in a relationship? Not long? What about 20 years down the road with a shared home and children? How do you manage your risk? It gets complicated fast.

Let's look at my basic method again, and I'll show you what I mean.

1. *Get in the game.* You know sure as hell that your future spouse is not going to show up and knock on your door. The odds are perhaps one in a billion. You know you must get out there, so you spiff up your looks, put on lipstick or shine your shoes, and off you go to the dance, the bar, the party, church, or work—wherever the game is being played. (In the case of Tinder, you take a good selfie and put yourself out there with a brilliant description. Yes, you are in the game.)

2. *Set clear goals.* Brilliant conversation or a good sense of humor? Sex with no strings attached? Marriage potential? A head turner? A big earner? Someone in your same religion or race? You know what you want. Of course, you've set goals for what you are looking for in a partner. If you haven't thought through these issues you are asking for trouble.

3. *Minimize your risk.* Would you take a date to see the most expensive show and eat at the most expensive restaurant in town on the first date? Probably not. But would you go out for coffee or drinks or Chinese

food with many promising candidates until you find the one who sets off a spark? Definitely. And you will most certainly use game theory by controlling the timing of your bets. Game theory uses observable facts to determine probability, right? So, if there is no one who meets your goals, you'd rather "sit this one out," rather than investing good time and money on a date you already know is going to be a dud, right? This is a clarifying way of thinking for many of life's confusing situations.

4. *Cut your losses quickly, and let your winnings run.* You will give marriage vast amounts of time, money, and energy—despite the odds that the chances of divorce are fifty-fifty. Early on especially, it's important that you don't drain your resources on bad bets.

LOVE AND TREND FOLLOWING: THE PATH TO MARRIAGE AS A SERIES OF BETS

Where would you place your bets in each of these scenarios?

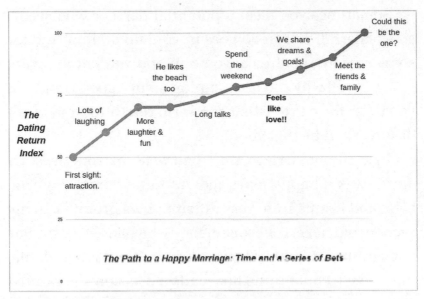

FIGURE 4.2 **Love and Trend Following: Run with Your Wins**

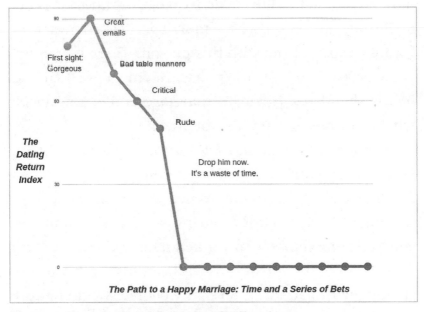

FIGURE 4.3 **Love and Trend Following: Cut Your Losers**

Sometimes you meet a potential partner who seems so wonderful. The trend goes up and up and up, and for some reason, this freaks you out, and you cut and run. Ask yourself why you are jumping off of a good trend. Do you think life can't be that good? Do you think you do not deserve for it be that good?

In my first marriage, the trend went up from the start and it was a happy marriage. As I mentioned, my wife Sybil and I came from very different backgrounds. In my second marriage, I chose someone who had a very similar background to mine. Sharon is from Brooklyn and, like me, came from nothing but made a decision she wanted a better life. She was also friend of Sybil's. Because we had so much in common, there was so much that she understood that I didn't need to explain. Marriage is one of life's biggest bets. On each marriage, I asked myself, do I want to spend time with this person? There is so much you have to do with your spouse. Having a great time in bed is chemistry. Having a marriage is life. You decide what you want to count as worthwhile.

See where I am going? *Let your winners run.* Getting into and staying in a good relationship is much easier than getting out of one. When do we cut losses in a marriage? A friendship? A business? Just as with money, you must ask yourself how much money you are willing to lose. So many fortunes have been lost in history by sticking with bad ideas. So many people stay in bad situations waiting it out despite all evidence that the trend is sinking. People start a business and hang on for 5 or 10 years despite poor returns.

Years ago, a young woman I had known since childhood told me her growing fear about going to work every morning at the high school she taught at in the Bronx. We were walking on the beach one day when she told me what she really wanted to do was be a therapist.

"Why aren't you?" I asked.

"I don't want to give up my pension."

But then she went on to describe a horrifying event. A few weeks earlier, a student upset about failing a course walked up to a colleague of hers, a fellow teacher, and shot the teacher point-blank in the face.

"Wait," I said. "You're telling me you are working in a place where one kid can shoot another or shoot you, and you don't want to leave because of a pension?" What is a pension compared to the risk of getting shot? It's a bad trade. First of all, there is no guarantee you are going to get the pension—because so many things can happen between now and then. And you can get shot and lose your life risking it daily to keep the supposedly "safe" job rather than pursue her lifelong passion of earning a graduate degree in clinical psychology.

Thankfully she came to see she needed to cut her losses by following the rule. She quit the job, went to school, and went on to have a successful career as a psychologist.

People find it so difficult to walk away from sunk costs. If you stay too focused too long on a bad bet, you are going to miss better opportunities. This can be said for the markets as well as in life.

In the same way, don't buy into the myth that walking away makes you a quitter. If you're running for US president and trailing badly in the primaries, don't hang around to show you're the real thing when you can't possibly win and do stupid stuff that only makes the rest of your life miserable. Remember your goal: You want to be US president. Come back in four years with a better plan.

Remember, there are so many things we cannot control in life and markets. But you do have control over the choices you make. And you can make a conscious decision about how much you are willing to lose. I take you back to the initial questions: Who are you? What do you want? With a trend following mindset, you empower yourself to see with clarity that you can make the right choice for right now. Trend following gives any motivated person a chance to invest in the markets with managed risk.

5

How to Lose Money, Including How I Lost Millions

The other day I was at the gym and saw a guy at the punching bag, working hard, throwing the most ineffectual punches I ever saw. Now, I don't know anything about how to throw a good punch except that, like most people, I've heard somewhere you've got to "put your whole body into it." I had no idea what that meant until I watched this guy thrusting his arm forward and back like a lever, without any force. Suddenly it became clear to me why his efforts produced a fraction of the power they could have. He was doing it all wrong. I almost felt I could go correct him, though of course I didn't. I just watched as he continued, blissfully ignorant, exhausting himself, making the same mistake over and over.

So often we are blind to ourselves. Our ego, fear, and yearnings keep us from seeing the mistakes we are making, even when they are plain as day. We want to avoid taking a loss, so we hang on and deceive ourselves that things will soon turn around. We put ourselves at serious risk and cling to false realities. I should know because it has happened to me. There was a time in my life when I was flying so high I didn't see the punch coming right at me. As a result, I lost millions and nearly destroyed my life.

How to get rich is always a very popular topic. But if you are in the markets, it is more important to learn how to lose money and not how to lose so big that you get wiped out in a moment. Why? Aspirations fight against reality. That's fine. But we must also understand the pitfalls and threats. Sometimes we can see mistakes more clearly. Over the years, I have watched so many people lose fortunes (including myself), and it comes down to one thing, which is just the opposite of the rule I've given you. Instead of cutting your losses short and letting your profits run, people who lose a lot freeze when they have a setback. Their small losses turn into deep holes, like someone with a shovel who keeps digging while water fills the bottom and they can't swim. I am alive financially because I cut my losses and became wealthy because I let my winners run.

I've collected eight of the most popular ways for you to lose money. Study well. If I were still a stand-up comic,

I might perform these with a laugh drumbeat *ba-dum* after each. If you're wondering which of these mistakes led me to lose millions, you'll have to wait until the end. Number 8 is mine.

EIGHT WAYS TO LOSE MONEY

1. Be a Genius

You know the wunderkid who dazzled his teachers, graduated magna cum laude, and had an IQ that could boil water? Of course he thinks he's special—because he is. Being a genius has given him so many advantages and so much praise. But the genius who goes to the best schools and achieves higher and higher status each year of life can face disadvantages in the market. For one thing, the market doesn't care about how smart you are. It isn't impressed by your grades or degrees. Remember, success in stocks, bonds, and commodities is not like figure skating where you get some points for executing difficult moves. In the markets only the final result counts, and it can be zero. That means you can be right *most of the time*, but still lose everything if you put too much on one wrong bet. The market won't even say it's sorry. I have observed that sometimes it's the Ivy League people most of all who hang on to their losses to the point of self-destruction because they cannot comprehend that after all of their education they are just wrong.

2. Assume the Market Owes You Money

I had a friend who made a great deal of money on sugar and got rich. But then he lost a lot of money on sugar. How did that happen? For the longest time, he had this idea that he had to get a big win in sugar. Why? Because sugar supposedly owed him money. He then kept betting on sugar for years but nothing ever came of it. Then one day, I noticed that sugar finally made a big leap. I called my friend and asked how it had gone for him, fully expecting to hear joy. But instead, his voice hesitated. "I missed the day to go in." He had been so sure that sugar would make him whole again that he wasn't paying attention to the actual facts. He wasn't in it at the moment of right now.

3. Ignore the Trend

Think about another example. The market for corn is sinking (it could be Apple stock or Bitcoin—for my example it doesn't matter). Now you should go and buy a lot of corn at this new cheaper price, because it's bound to go up again?

Wrong.

Yes, of course, you may get a great opportunity to buy after a sell-off, but to think this is a blanket rule would be a terrible mistake. Some stocks sink for very good reasons. You don't want to buy them. For example, horse and buggy materials fell in value after the arrival of the car.

Would you do well if you ran out and bought more stock in a saddle-making company?

Let me put it this way. If you go to Brooklyn, would you get on a train to the Bronx first? I did that once, and I can tell you it is not what you want to do. I was on my way to Brooklyn, which is south of Manhattan, after a meeting where every thought I'd uttered was praised. I must be a genius, I thought, as I sat on the subway car, rattling from one stop to the next. Suddenly, I looked up and realized that the train was heading to the Bronx, not Brooklyn. Despite being a New Yorker all my life, riding the subways by myself since age nine, I'd gotten on the wrong train.

Ask yourself frequently if your vision is corresponding to reality. If you buy a stock or commodity for a dollar, thinking it's going to go up, and the next time you look it's at 90 cents, be real with yourself. You did something wrong. Get out. And don't feel bad either. It doesn't mean you're wrong forever. It just means you were wrong this time. Move on to the next opportunity to be right.

4. Failure to Get out of a Bad Position

You have the deal of the century looking at you. You think the odds are 95 percent in your favor, so you put down a really big bet, with the thrill of envisioning how much you can win.

Then a sad thing happens. You are in the 5 percent who loses. Now you may have to sell your house, trade down your car, and deliver bad news to your kid who was planning to attend a private college. Are you ready to do this? If not, then bet only what you can afford to lose. In fact, "How much can I lose?" should be your first question, *not* "How much can I win?" (Repeat this like a mantra.)

5. Hang on When You're Losing

Years ago, my cousin turned $5,000 into $100,000 in the options market. I asked him how he did it.

"It's easy," he explained. "I buy an option and if it goes up, I stay in, but if it goes down, I don't get out until I am at least even."

I tried to warn him that his strategy wasn't going to work all the time. It was far too risky. But he didn't listen. He used $100,000 to buy options of Merrill Lynch stock for very cheap. It was all the money he had, but he wasn't worried a bit. He assured me that the options had hit bottom and had to go up and soon he'd be making a killing.

"There's going to be a killing," I said, "but the face you see on the killing floor is gonna be yours."

He stuck to his guns. "Even if they go up 10 percent, I'll make 200 percent on my investment."

But in fact, the price never went back up, and he told me he lost $110,000.

I told him, "How can this be? It's impossible to lose more than you put in. Where is that extra $10,000 from?"

He replied, "Oh, I didn't tell you?" he said. "I borrowed another $10,000 from the bank."

I was astonished to learn that when he was losing, he borrowed even more money to buy more options. There was zero evidence that he was right, but he was bucking the trend on borrowed money and risked more than he could afford to lose. Why? In our mind hope is valued differently than losing. This is also why people in bad marriages stay, and based on my experience, this is how most fortunes are lost.

6. Be a Winner

Another friend of mine was a great athlete and good looking. He did well in school and he was not used to losing. In fact, he never lost at anything. His parents spoiled him and bought him a Corvette when he was 16 years old. He didn't know how to prepare for loss, prevent loss, or cope with loss. He bought stocks, and when they went down, he stayed with them and held on. Those stocks never came back. At age 70 he wound up being supported by his kids.

People used to winning are far less likely to acknowledge they are actually losing. They will hang on longer to their losing bets. Because I'd been a poor athlete and bad student, it never surprised me that I would lose. I would quickly accept it, fold my cards, and move on to come back to play another day. I recommend you *practice* losing money. In the long run, that will help you win big.

7. Get Confused at What Your Objective Is

You spot a rising trend. Say, the 30-day average price for apartment buildings in a certain neighborhood has been going up for a year. You decide to buy an apartment building because you believe it will go up in value and you can make a killing. Soon, you fall in love with the building because it has a beautiful lobby designed by a famous architect. You tell yourself that a great lobby makes it more valuable.

In fact, you've just lost your objectivity. You didn't buy the building for the lobby, you bought it for the rent roll. You need to be looking at the condition of the building and whether rents are rising. Be objective and tear yourself away from that lobby love.

8. Be Arrogant

Losing all your money and getting wiped out is one thing. Losing all your money plus millions of dollars other people have entrusted you with is quite another thing. When the mistake happened, I was not the one who made the original error. But it was my fault for not seeing it coming. It was my fault for not discovering it once it was in play. I was too big for that. Business was going great, and I was on top of the world. I had other guys who were working on the ground implementing and managing money. As I saw it, I was the concept guy who flew on jets around the world, making deals. I was above looking closely at what was really going on. And I didn't check. When I got numbers, I believed them. My arrogance led to this, and it was nearly a fatal flaw. Here is what happened to me. I hope my story can prevent you from making a similar mistake.

HOW I LOST EVERYTHING

The partnership I'd created in the mid-seventies was a commodities options market maker, which meant, in simple terms, we acted as a clearinghouse that bought and sold commodities options for our own account and for customer accounts. It required huge reserves of cash. I'd started with funding from a Swiss bank, which was holding the collateral. The trading went very well and we continued to get customers.

The thing about a market maker is that everything had to be hedged. That is to say, if we agreed to buy a billion dollars of options, we always backed them up by finding a buyer for a billion dollars of options. The differ-ence in the buy-sell price was our profit, and the hedge was our safety.

When customers bought into our fund, they invested a minimum amount of cash up front and agreed on a margin of three times that amount in reserve. So, for example, a customer put up $50,000 in cash, but pledged another $150,000 if the company needed it.

By then, I had a partner working with me. He was a quant who helped me test and run our trading system. I was the outside guy, and he was the inside guy who managed the books. I always needed people to execute my ideas. It was part of being dyslexic and blind. I needed eyes to see for me. I needed people who could work with numbers who were not dyslexic, but who were bright and could mathematically see what I wanted to do after I explained it to them. My partner was that guy, and I liked him. He had a nice wife and kids. He'd started for me the way everyone started working for me, with a stake in the company instead of a salary, because when I was starting out, I had no money. Over time, it paid off for him and he was doing very well.

We were so successful that Simon, my attorney, convinced me to move my residence and business operations to New Jersey to save on taxes. When I'd been promoting rock concerts, I'd passed through Summit, New Jersey, and was amazed by how green it was. My wife Sybil and I decided to move there to start our family. I took an office on the ninth floor of the Gateway Building in Newark. Simon was on the fourteenth.

It was an exciting time. Our market maker company took off, raising $5 million and then $10 million that I was trading. Then we formed another company to use the same strategy we'd used in commodities but applied to the bond and treasury markets. This raised another $10 million.

I enjoyed those years because I was creating new and out-of-the-box ways to make money, which is what I most love to do. For example, when I heard that Dr. Richard Sandor—then the chief economist of the Chicago Board of Trade—had developed the first futures contract on government interest rates, I told Simon I wanted to do it. "We can do well at this," I said.

"Larry, that's genius, but we don't know how," Simon said.

"Well, why don't I call Dr. Sandor and find out about it?"

"Do you know him?"

"No. I don't know him."

"How the hell are you going to meet with him?"

"I'm going to get on a plane and walk into his office," I explained. Simon was often surprised at the way I could call anybody up. I don't know how to explain it, but I've always been able to do this. Maybe it is my comfort with failure. What's the worst thing someone can do? Turn me away?

A couple of days later, I was in Dr. Sandor's office. Sandor was a brilliant man and we had a great conversation. (He turned out to be a kid from Brooklyn, too.) With his insights, we went ahead and started trading interest rate futures.

• • •

In November 1979, everything changed.

Inflation had been racing up for much of the decade and now was over 11 percent. Paul Volcker, who'd recently become head of the Federal Reserve, had launched a war against inflation. He'd begun a campaign of interest rate hikes. Our customers were anticipating big movements and came running to us to place their positions in our market maker fund.

But that November, Simon got a phone call from my partner.

"I have to come up and talk to you," my partner said. "And after I do, then I'm going to jump out of the window."

Whether Simon believed him or not, I do not know. But it was an attention-getter for sure.

Simon wouldn't meet until I got there. I arrived within the hour, and the three of us met in Simon's office. When the door shut behind us, my partner delivered the news.

"I didn't hedge," he said. "I'm sorry. I opened one side for a billion and didn't hedge it . . ." His voice was calm. He said something about Volcker's interest rates and that we were left *without* a lot of money. He didn't know how much.

I had to unwind his words. Somehow I got out the question: "Why?"

"Because I thought Volker would stop raising rates."

For years after this, I would reflect on my partner's decision to override our system on his own without consultation with me or anyone else. Was it ego or greed or fear that led him to risk everything? I never knew for sure. He was a very smart guy with a high IQ who had gone on scholarship to an elite college. He was handsome and had a lovely family. Now his life would never be the same.

It turned out my partner had made this mistake quite a bit earlier but had been hiding it from me, covering over it with other trades. Certainly, every day he looked at it, it had become worse, and every day he'd become paralyzed with more fear. I tell people all the time: The first loss is the best—because you can get out quickly. That is not what happened. Instead of facing the loss and crossing it out that day, he panicked. He knew better, but he was emotionally hoping that somehow, someway, he would get *saved*. Another person in the firm was assigned to check the books, but as I later learned, my partner had misdirected and intimidated him. So it had all been hidden.

Simon and I were wiped out. He had brought some of his law partners and clients into the fund, and now they could be wiped out, too, along with our friends and scores of other customers. We believed we could all go bankrupt. We owed to the government, brokers, banks, and several huge financial firms. "Oh my God," my partner said. "They're going to kill us. Now I'm going to jump out the window."

Fortunately the windows were locked. I think he *would* have done it if he could have. We were in shock. However, the way my brain works is to immediately look for *survival*. I was clearly up a tree and the tree was on fire, but I was looking for branches that were not yet in flames so I could climb down. I remember thinking that Simon's law firm was totally screwed and so they'd have to help me get out of this.

For the next few days we didn't sleep. When the dust settled, we could see our position. We owed $7 million more than what we had.

Unfortunately, I had to continue to work with my partner to sort things out. You might wonder how I managed to be in the same room with someone who had deceived me and caused such profound losses. Well, it was very simple. I divide my life into goals. What I like doesn't matter. What I have to do matters. I had to submerge my feelings. My partner was the one who managed the books, and I had to work with him to solve our problems.

When a friend asked me to describe how upset I was, I said, "You know, six point nine doesn't bother me that much, but the hundred really hurts." Humor went only so far. On most mornings during this period, the first thing I did when I woke up was to vomit.

By then, my father had lost his business, and I was supporting him as I had been raised to do. I called to tell him about what had happened. "Look, Dad. I'm not sure I can keep this up, because I owe millions more than I have," I said. "One guy alone I owe $4 million. I mean that's a problem."

"No," my father replied. "It's not your problem. It's his problem."

There was a brilliance to this. I learned the power of the weak position shortly thereafter when one guy decided to get tough and yell at me. I told him to stop, that he couldn't threaten me because I was already dead. This was effective.

We decided on a course of action. My trades had at least done well, so we at least had some cash to put toward our debts, albeit a drop in the bucket compared to the magnitude of what we owed. Remember this: If you owe someone money, you can offer what you have in cash, and try to negotiate away the rest. People want their money and they might take half now rather than nothing later. We owed money to three very major financial firms, and two negotiated with us.

While we negotiated and held at bay the financial firms, I did extremely well with the long silver and gold positions I was able to keep open. Our negotiations with the financial firms turned out quite favorably, if you can call losing double of all our money "favorable." But at least we were not facing the losses of three or four times of everything we had that we were originally facing.

After the financial firms, Simon and I went to see in person every single one of our investors. Out of 100 investors, 98 agreed to meet with us. Then we told them what we had done to limit the losses and we "only" had to ask them for a third of the margin they'd pledged (which was double what they'd originally invested) so we could stay in the game and win back their money. All but two agreed.

I had to work with the lawyers, accountants, and investors to keep the creditors at bay, trying not to get sued. I remember going to California to visit one of our investors who made about $10 million a year. He had a huge estate in the countryside and a large staff of workers. When we made our request, he looked at me and said, "You got a pair of balls on you. Normally if someone came in here and wanted another million dollars, I would turn my fucking dogs on him. I'm not going to give you any money. But I'm not going to turn the dogs on you."

Around this time, the IRS started to investigate a trader who worked with our company. I learned that we were his biggest client. As I said earlier, our tax shelters were legal, and when we'd built the structure, I'd paid attorneys to write tax opinions that explained why it was legal. I might have gotten close to the line, but I never wanted to cross it or do anything illegal. I didn't know what he'd done wrong, but I knew the way the feds made cases was to get people to turn in their friends and clients. I was terrified that he'd somehow blame me, and I'd be going to jail.

I had to tell my wife Sybil about it. She was pregnant with our first child and had just learned that we had no money. Now I had to tell her that I might be facing jail time.

She stood silent, taking it in. Then in her composed British manner she said, "Your kind always has a scheme." She turned and went up the stairs. That's the last thing she ever said about it.

In fact, she was right. I could have gotten a job and left the whole thing as a giant mess. Instead, I came up with a *scheme*. I looked at my debt and decided to go back and do what I really liked. I wanted to create an improved trading system that would remove human discretion entirely. Clearly I couldn't trust humans. So I decided to pull myself up and start all over. Some people are born with this kind of persistence, and other people build it up through practice. Either way, if you are going to be investing or trying to do anything big in life, you have to be able to take a hit, get up, and stand strong again. If there is one thing that made me successful in life, it has been this persistence. But I must admit, this time was no doubt the most challenging of all. Somehow I knew I had to come back even bigger. I started creating a new plan.

PART II

THE MINT FUND, MARKET WIZARDS, AND LIVING THE RULE

6

Making Mint: Know Where You Are Playing the Game

had a big idea, but I was broke and needed income. Luckily, an opportunity arose to help a client in California with strategies to mitigate tax liabilities. My percentage on this was $100,000, and it was enough to cover my family and business expenses for a long while (I'd always been an underspender). I had no idea exactly how long that would be. I was busy with non-income-producing activities—cleaning up the trouble made by my partner and working on a new venture.

My goal was to create a scientific trading system that would remove human emotion from buying and selling decisions and rely instead on a purely statistical approach built on preset rules. To pull it off, I needed to find a new partner with the formal training to build a model and rigorously test all of my ideas. A friend of mine introduced me to his brother-in-law, Peter Matthews, who was then in his late twenties, finishing a PhD in statistics at American University. Peter was doing consulting work for the federal government but was interested in trading futures. He came out to my office in Newark for a meeting, and I told him that I just couldn't trust the human element anymore and was looking for someone to create an automated system that would make money. Then I had to convince him that he should join this venture even though I had no funds to pay him. I said, "If it works, you will share in the profits and be a partner." He was extremely bright and at an age where he could take this kind of risk. He said yes.

Building an automated trading system was a major undertaking circa 1980. We knew of no one else doing this at the time. (In fact, I now know that Ed Seykota and others had started in the seventies.) There were no clear books or informative guides to follow. We also needed access to mainframe computers that could process huge volumes of data.

With these hurdles in place Peter began designing our trading trend following approach. He wrote algorithms to monitor moving price averages across many commodities, identify rising trends, computerize the odds that those trends would continue, filtering out trades that had too much risk, and trigger automated buying and selling actions when our particular conditions were met. In this era it was extremely tedious work (you can do it on your phone now). Peter was able to use the computers at American University at night, but even so it was slow going. His painstaking process also included checking his calculations by hand. There were moments when I did wonder if this could all work!

From the start, I wanted our system to be agnostic to whatever market we were trading. This was an unusual philosophy at the time, but ever since I'd moved from pork bellies to corn to coffee, I'd come to believe that human behaviors more or less are the same regardless of the particular market. Plus, by trading in so many types of markets we would get extreme diversification, which would help control risk. We also built in hedging rules, with system rules that went both long and short to protect against outsized losses.

After a year of painstaking design, Peter finished his work and brought in Michael Delman, an excellent computer programmer in his early twenties. (He began with us as a consultant but later became a junior partner.) Michael knew nothing of finance, but it didn't matter; his job was to backtest Peter's model to see if it would work on a larger scale. This involved buying and then inputting huge sets of historical trading data so that we could then run our model and see how it would have performed over past historical periods—not just one month or year, but across thousands of different markets and time periods. Now, obviously, just because you get something right in the past doesn't mean you will get it right in the future—historical testing has its flaws. Just the same, these simulations were highly valuable because using real market conditions—even in the past—gave us far better information than hypothetical scenarios of us sitting around the office guessing. The result: We scientifically proved it. Our trading system worked.

Over time, we continued to evolve and refine it. For example, we also tested various holding periods as a measure of our system performance. It seemed to us that evaluating performance on a calendar-year basis was an arbitrary measure. So Peter and Michael quantified the odds of profitable performance for time periods of different lengths. In our simulations, we found that 90 percent of all 6-month holding periods, 97 percent of 12-month periods, and 100 percent of 18-month periods were profitable.

All of these critical behind-the-scenes steps led to the founding of our company Mint Investment Management Company, which began trading in April 1981.

LONDON

Mint was born out of crisis, yes, but it was also born out of a fortuitous trip to London in 1981 to find new brokers.

Why London? It was expensive to operate in the United States. At that time, the tax rate was the highest in the world. Lawyers, investment bankers, and other middlemen took big commissions. And in 1981, a new law eliminated the tax structure I'd been using for many years. But also, other countries were more amenable to futures trading than the States. London was the new gateway to international financial markets right at the time when global trading was taking off. I went there to knock on doors.

At one appointment, I tried to set up a referral arrangement with a broker. I asked him if he would protect my commission if I sent clients to him. He wasted no time in saying no. It was a very short meeting. On my way out of his office, I stopped in the waiting room and picked up a magazine I'd been reading earlier and discretely ripped out an ad I'd seen for another commodities firm. I put it in my pocket. A little later, I called the number and spoke with David Anderson, who agreed to meet me.

It's interesting to look back at this moment. If I had been the kind of person who was unaccustomed to failure, perhaps I would have brooded my way out of the office after that rejection. But being who I was, I immediately began thinking about my next move—hence, ripping out that ad. In many ways, this gesture was a small act of trend following. When one trend isn't working, don't hang on, just get out and look for the next opportunity.

Or going back to my romance analogy: If you have a bad date, do you stop dating and become a monk?

The phone call to David Anderson changed my life. He was a leader in London's futures trading world. He was also associated with ED&F Man, the elite global commodities merchant and trading firm. Anderson and Man had recently launched a joint venture: Anderson Man Limited. It was Man's first step into the commodities futures market, and Anderson had helped open that door. He also opened the door for my partners and me.

We created an "advisor" relationship with Man and put our trading system to work in dozens of markets around the world. We carried out our business in the same US offices, using our hands-off statistical system that had been backtested and proven. When the system kicked out its recommendations, we sent the trades to Man, who executed them in London.

My partners and I had the right combination of complementary abilities. I was the idea person who also went out and did deals. Michael once said I had 20 ideas a week. Peter was the statistical mind who managed the trading program and performed analytics. And Michael executed all of the computer work and made sure the trains ran on time. In our first two years, we made more than 20 percent annually. People started to take notice. However, we still didn't have the level of business that I wanted and needed. It was still hard to sell our style of funds in the first place. For our first few years at Mint, most people wouldn't even talk to me. Plus, when I would explain that we traded coffee and gold the same way, they would get off the phone. Sometimes they would hang up. Today, systematic trading is more accepted, but back then it was unknown, untrusted, and unwanted by the masses. Again, being a dyslexic kid accustomed to failure, what did I care? I just picked myself up and went on to my next call and my next potential opportunity.

ED&F Man, however, had vast capital, reputation, and global connections. In 1983, I met with the chairman and told him I wanted Man to buy a stake in Mint. He was reluctant. Man was a very particular upper-class elite culture. The company had been founded in the eighteenth century as a sugar trader, and for some 200 years it did business with the British Navy. It was the world's oldest commodity trading house, with agents all around the world who brokered deals from Europe to the Congo. Man's clients were primarily giant manufacturers and governments. Our small company, Mint, on the other hand, was a commodity trading advisor (CTA). That meant we advised individual investors to buy, sell, and hedge in markets with techniques that some still saw as the Wild West—and from his perspective, perhaps a bit unseemly. He and his colleagues also had trouble believing that a computerized method could possibly be better than human judgment. Still, Man wanted to get in the futures markets, and so I made him an offer that was hard to refuse: a 50 percent stake in Mint in exchange for paying the salaries of my partners and me for five years, free access to their mainframe computers, and a $5 million line of credit to get us started.

It was a great deal for us because Man had the banking connections, money, and computers that I couldn't afford. It was a good deal for him because Man got a chance to make a lot of money in a fast-growing field. Commodities futures were taking off, and not many players had a legitimate strategy to trade them and manage risk.

He said yes. Now we could take off.

• • •

You always want to know *where* you are when playing the game. In many ways, England was the best for me. As I began flying over there, I assumed the role of a cultural anthropologist. We all speak English, I said to myself. Now I've just got to figure out what they mean. I learned early on that sometimes when my British colleagues said one thing, they meant the exact opposite. (Being married to a Brit wasn't much preparation. She was a very sincere person and wasn't like my colleagues, because she wasn't of their class.)

I learned on the ground and came to like the people at Man. They were polite and some of the smartest associates I ever worked with. In many ways, it was a place made for me. Anti-Semitism was widespread in England at the time, but far less present at Man, and once I proved myself, it faded away. I discovered that my colleagues in England really wanted to make money

Of course, as the Brooklyn guy, I was a bit more aggressive than they were used to. I remember one time being at a meeting with a big long table, and there were phones all about because it was a brokerage firm. I was meeting with the lawyer who represented one of the country's major exchanges, perhaps it was the cocoa exchange. He was very British, and I was trying to convince him to change a rule. I made a strong case and then said, "It will benefit everyone."

"Well, I'll pen a letter to so and so . . ."

Now I had just flown in on the Concorde jet. I reached over and picked up the phone and held it out.

"Call him," I said. An Englishman never would have done that. But a kid from Brooklyn could be direct like this. To be sure, there were also times when I held back to make my more reserved colleagues more comfortable. This is why I say you need to know where you are playing the game. You need to understand the rules and perspectives of the other players in their culture. If you adapt yourself to the place, you improve your odds. Though I liked the people, I never liked the politics. If you are this way also, then pay especially close attention to the rules of engagement in the place where you are working. Using those rules to your advantage is your responsibility.

Man had been a cash commodity firm, which is a business built heavily on credit, and so it had excellent relationships with bankers and hired many ex-bankers into its ranks. This opened doors for Mint—big time. Through Man, I could do business in the Middle East, Europe, Australia, and Japan—basically all over the world. Even so, convincing people about our trading still took some persuasion. For example, I got a meeting with a venerable old financial firm in Australia where no one had ever done a fund like ours. I explained how our system worked and asked them to hold bonds for us and guarantee them. Usually once you make the sale, the other firm gets a commission and it's over; they are unemployed. But I told my counterpart that if they would work with us, they'd get money for guaranteeing, and instead of selling once for one commission, they'd be getting money all the time. This got his attention.

By 1988, we registered an average annual com-pounded return of over 30 percent since our 1981 founding. During that time our best year was 60 percent growth (1987, the year of a stock market crash), and our worst year was plus 13 percent. We were by then receiv-ing a lot of attention in the business media, including a 1986 "best of" award from *Businessweek.* Jack Schwager then profiled me in his 1989 book, *Market Wizards.*

Soon, I was on a rhythm going on the Concorde, mak-ing the three-and-a-half-hour flight from New York to London regularly. I flew over on Sunday night and worked there and traveled through Europe during the week. Then on Friday afternoon I got back on the Concorde to fly home and see my wife and kids. I flew so much that one year they gave me a leather pilot's jacket. By 1990, less than 10 years after we started, we were the biggest hedge fund in the world with a record-breaking $1 billion under management.

ASYMMETRICAL LEVERAGE AND THE GUARANTEED FUND: OUR WINNING FORMULA

One of the biggest engines behind our success was a risk management concept I called asymmetrical leverage (AL). AL is how I got rich and how you can too. Essentially it means that what you risk and what you can gain are of dramatically different weights. Or as I like to think of it, you bet pennies, but you can potentially win dollars. Asymmetrical leverage can be especially important for people or organizations in a weaker position (think David and Goliath).

Our big asymmetrical idea came out of a London cocktail party. Lord Stanley Fink (later to become CEO of the Man Group), David Anderson, and other directors of Man excelled at social networking and getting to know the right people (those with money to invest). I was out with them one night at an event Man sponsored and started chatting with a guy who, it turned out, was a high-net-worth investor.

"Your returns are impressive," he told me. "But my current manager is getting close to that and your fees are higher. You are charging 2 percent of the management fee and 20 percent of the profits. They are taking no management fee—just 20 percent of profits. Why should I invest with you?"

I went home and thought about what he said. I could see his point. I wondered, "How can I do this? How can I lure more investors to Mint?" This was 1985, and by now, I had two kids and a house. Man was getting 50 percent of all profits, and I was also sharing with my other partners. I was motivated to do better.

I spoke with my partners about the idea of a "no lose" fund. What if we could take 60 percent of an investor's money and put it in zero-coupon, five-year US Treasury bonds where it would not only be perfectly safe but would also double in about five years' time? (Remember, this was the 1980s when interest rates were very high.)

Then we'd take the other 40 percent of the investor's money and invest it in our trading program. Worst-case scenario, we lose everything in systems, but we could still return the entire principal within five years (and cover our management fees). In other words, we could say to an investor: Give us a million now and you are guaranteed that you will, at minimum, get a million back after five years. The only thing you'd lose was the time value of the money. What you could win, however, was a major capital gain because our trading system was delivering stellar results year after year. We called it the "Mint Guaranteed Ltd. Fund." When we first announced the fund, it was highly publicized in places such as the *New York Times,* for example. Some coverage suggested it was too good to be true, including one reporter at a major British paper who ridiculed the new fund—on the same page, the paper ran a separate article about Ponzi schemes. His implication about our fund was clear. (The executives at Man considered suing the paper for libel but decided instead to invite the editor in for lunch and clear the air.) Nonetheless, the guaranteed fund took off, and we made $75 million in our first year.

I look for asymmetrical opportunities all the time and suggest you do the same for all aspects of your life. When I sold ED&F Man on our merger, I was offering them asymmetrical leverage—though I didn't call it that at the time. A few years later, I wrote a white paper for my partners at the Man Group explaining the philosophical and financial phenomenon of what we'd done. No one has read this analysis outside of a few partners until you.

In the paper I summed up the principles underlying the asymmetrical leverage of Mint's merger with the Man Group. Here is a brief excerpt:

> AL [asymmetrical leverage] is unique in that it affords one the benefits of conventional leverage minus the proportional risk. . . .

The Man acquisition is an example of good AL for both sides. Man was worth over $100 million at the time and its risk was only $750,000, a small percentage of Man's net worth. They had the opportunity to buy 50 percent of Mint at a less than 5 percent chance of losing their $750,000, which set their real risk at $40,000, with a large body of statistical evidence showing them that they could not lose.

From the Hite, Delman, and Matthews (HMD) side we received the best AL factors possible: time and money. We got five years and the use of several million dollars for our own account plus an absolute income floor.

The structural factors that supported the initial partnership were:

a. Predetermined probabilities in trading risk; and
b. The fact that futures margins paid T-bill rates and Man was able to borrow under prime, making financing cheap.

These are the same factors that make our guarantee deals work. They allowed us to risk $250,000 out of a cash flow of two million at the time we launched the first guaranteed fund, which will earn us over 50 million by the end of this year. This will give us a return of 40 times our original investment of $250,000, which was 12.5 percent of our then cash flow.

I wrote the paper to get my partners fired up about a proposal for a new strategy using asymmetrical leverage. I used a number of examples such as Mint's arrangement with a Middle Eastern financial institution. We built a $15 million Islamic portfolio for their investors, earning 23 percent of the profit per month while risking none of Mint's money.

In all I've learned then and since, three ingredients make up the secret sauce of asymmetrical leverage—ingredients that led the Mint Fund to become the largest commodity trading advisor in the world. Anyone can understand the ingredients and apply them to different business, investing, policy, and life situations.

The First Ingredient Is Time

Often in life (but not always) the faster you move, the better. But with time to identify the best opportunities, you can improve your odds. Now I have talked about this in a previous chapter, but let's take a closer look at how powerful time is as an element of asymmetrical leverage. With the guaranteed fund, we made investors wait five years. Time is an especially powerful form of leverage in growing money. With time, we could take advantage of bond maturity and a good long stretch of trading opportunity. Though five years was a relatively long time, investors were willing to give it to us because of what we offered in exchange—a dream combination of no-risk profit.

The Second Is Knowledge

If you don't know the odds, you can't make an intelligent bet. If you've read the book this far, you're conversant with the importance of knowing the odds for any decision. But there's a role for knowing the game, as well. In Mint, I brought knowledge from a decade's experience in trading. I also brought in bright partners who contributed essential knowledge of statistics and computers that other traders weren't yet using. Without them, there would have been no Mint. By now I definitely had learned to trust.

One of the greatest (and most famous) examples of knowledge-powered asymmetrical leverage is found in the success story of the Oakland A's under the management of Billy Beane—as told in Michael Lewis's book *Moneyball* and the movie starring Brad Pitt. When Beane became general manager of the A's in late 1997, it was one of the worst teams in baseball with one of the lowest payrolls. Up until then, most baseball scouts used subjective criteria for drafting their talent. They looked for players who possessed a combination of qualities, such as having "the face" (i.e., a handsome visage), a 99 mph "heater," or a "can't-miss swing." Beane believed this was all bullcrap. He knew you could measure performance by numbers and revolutionized the game by pioneering a statistical approach to acquiring talent.

If you've read the book or seen the film, you know that one of the most important decisions Beane ever made was to hire an assistant general manager who had an economics degree from Harvard. Beane and Paul DePodesta introduced the analytical principles of sabermetrics to analyze player performance. Many players overlooked by other teams, and who could be signed for lower salaries, possessed skills that were not in vogue—getting on base, hitting for power whether or not the hitter struck out frequently. The A's piled up incremental advantages of high on-base average and slugging for power to outperform many teams that paid top-tier free agents. Analytics showed that two players who make vastly different sums can generate equivalent production. That was Beane's asymmetrical leverage.

By recruiting unconventional sources of knowledge, Beane says he was able to make "rational objective decisions in a business where everybody was making subjective decisions." The Oakland A's made the playoffs eight times between 1999 and 2014. Beane did this with a small payroll but outsized knowledge.

Today, every team in baseball, and even the National Basketball Association (NBA) too, has adopted an analytics approach. As a result, Beane's asymmetrical leverage has waned because other teams began using similar strategies.

But his numbers revolution did not wane. Beane then exploited asymmetrical leverage in a different way and began questioning the game's conventional use of a single pitcher to play seven or eight innings of a nine-inning game. Faced with a long history of devastating injuries to starting pitchers, a relatively thin national talent pool for starting pitcher prospects, and the huge amount of salary pitchers demand, teams were gradually embracing a new model of keeping individual pitch counts under 100 per game to protect the arms of starting pitchers. The best medical research pointed in this direction. Beane and a few other executives realized this was a long trend, a likely permanent shift in the game. Beane invested in the "back end" of his pitching staff with more and better relievers. Because the game's history had long established a view of relief pitchers as having lesser status and value than starting pitchers and "aces," their salaries were cheaper. Beane's knowledge of analytics and more emotionally detached approach to the game gave him new asymmetrical leverage. He spent less on starters and invested more on top-quality relievers, who would control far more of the game than in the past. The A's continue to be one of the best stories in baseball, thanks to a management approach that leveraged a unique type of knowledge and strategy that no one else was using.

The Third Ingredient Is Money (Not Your Own Money— Other People's Money)

Money buys you time, buys you knowledge, and allows the long-terms odds to work in your favor. Money leverages the advantages of the first two ingredients. In the case of the guaranteed fund, we leveraged money that was not our own—money provided by the US Treasury in the form of interest paid on a five-year bond. As I mentioned earlier, using OPM (other people's money) provides great leverage in building wealth. We built Mint using the start-up money provided by ED&F Man.

In 1994, Man became a public company. Man and Mint parted ways and the British era of my life ended—at least for a time. But after 20 years of managing other people's money, I didn't want to have to answer to political interests, and working in a public company would only bring more people to please.

I wanted to execute my own ideas without having to ask permission or sell my ideas before I could test them. After 20 years as an asset manager, I simply wanted to manage my own money, research my ideas, and advise a few friends and supporters. If you have had the same job for 20 years, even if it has been a great boon, you probably have yearned for a fresh new challenge and a few less meetings. When the Man Group went public, Stanley Fink, who was then a CEO, wanted me to help him run the businesses. But I preferred the research side, not the operational side, and said no. That decision probably cost me $100,000,000, give or take a zero or two.

One of the earliest recommendations of this book is to know who you are. I have realized that I am happiest when I am independent and free to come up with new creative ideas to make money. In 1994, it was time to shift the game back to stateside and focus on managing my own money in a family office. In the final score, my partners and employees and I all did extremely well.

In your own way, in your own time, I want you to leverage that kind of success in your own life. You might not make $100,000,000, but if you make enough good bets, the odds will be in your favor in the long run. I realize that for many of my readers, the prospect of having $100,000 of seed money to start seems unlikely. In the next chapter, I will share step-by-step advice on applying my methods—steps that any investor can take.

7

How My Philosophy Can Work for You: Applications of the Rule

One of the great things about being successful is that you can then help others. However, when people ask me (as they do all the time) for stock tips and specific guidance on trades, I have to tell them that this is not how it works. My trading system cannot be shared piecemeal. My trading philosophy, on the other hand, most certainly can be applied to the benefit of the novice investor, the small investor, and the large investor, too. Since leaving Mint, I have found it very satisfying to talk to students and mentor young people on how to build wealth (don't worry, it's for you, too, if you are 50!).

For those interested in the basic mechanics of my trend following, I've shared it at the end of this chapter.

First things first.

WHERE DOES THE MONEY BEGIN?

As I mentioned in the previous chapter, I did an early deal in California and made $100,000, and these funds underwrote my family and business expenses for the period I was beginning Mint. Perhaps young investors might read this and feel that getting $100,000 together is beyond them—or that putting together even $10,000 is too difficult. I have two words for you: *want* and *count*.

1. Want

When it comes to getting your first investment money together, *want* is your most powerful word. Or if you prefer, *need*—because need converts to want. Remember, I had a wife and a baby on the way and no money. My need propelled me to that deal in California, and it had me knocking on doors in London. It is the power of your *want* that will drive you. There is not much more to say about this, except that you better look within yourself, or average is what you will get.

2. Count

You don't need to know advanced mathematics to make money. You simply need to count. You can build your first pile of money through counting.

You know I started with zero. But I saved up an initial $10,000 and then gathered investments from family and friends to build a pool of $100,000 I could trade with. I charged my investors a 20 percent fee for performance; this meant that if my fund earned 20 percent, for example, I would make 56 percent on my original investment of only 10 percent. In fact, I did much better. This is counting.

But where do you get that initial $10,000, you ask?

Count what you are making. Live on 90 percent of that and invest the other 10 percent. Seems obvious. You hear financial advisors say it all the time. Yet few people do it. Here's an example: Some of my friends counted on their annual bonuses as part of their salary. They used it to pay for things like a $30,000 bar mitzvah. But if you look up the word *bonus*, it is not part of salary—it's extra. And if you are living on your bonus, then chances are you are living on 110 percent of your salary. Not very good counting.

Another way to get started: Get a second job. Save $10,000 and bet $5,000. (Always be sure you have an emergency fund first before investing. An emergency fund can be three to six months' living expenses.)

The first time I realized this, I was a child at the beach with my cousin. We were going to sell ice cream, but I was too tired and lazy, so I quit and wandered about, waiting for my cousin's shift to be over. I found a poker game with other kids. I could barely see, but I counted

10 of them, and each put in a dollar. I thought to myself, I have a dollar, and if I watch the cards and count them, I have a chance at winning 10.

It's hard to believe you can make money just counting, but you can. Many businesses do exactly this: insurance, banks, and even advertising because they put out ads and use numeric profiles to track and test them. They count to see what works. Counting is what our computers did for us at Mint. I always wanted the computers running at night while we slept. As Warren Buffett once said, "If you don't find a way to make money while you sleep, you will work until you die."

I made a lot of money counting interest rates. In fact, so much of my success has been built on the smart use of debt and counting the difference between how much I am paying for money versus how much I am making from it. When I was in that college class and first heard my professor scoff at people who would put up 5 percent of the total trade in cash, everyone else was laughing. But I was counting, and that's how I figured out that with a mere $500 I could trade—and earn on—$10,000 in commodities.

Always count how much you have, how much you can lose, and how much you can make. Take the next bet, properly financed, when your counting tells you it makes sense. Remember this: Counting is a tool of thinking. Napoleon Hill said it, "You can think and grow rich."

What's the Difference Between a Good Gambler and a Poor One?

A good gambler keeps cutting his bets as he's losing.
A poor gambler keeps increasing, trying to catch up.

RISK CONTROL IS EVERYTHING

The market is not my friend. I do not know what it will do. I can control, however, how much I bet and when I bet. Cardinal rule number one, the name of this book: How much are you willing to lose? Do not pass Go, or make a single trade, or bet anything at all until you answer this question. Only you can know yourself, your resources, and your temperament for loss. But no matter what, never bet your lifestyle. Here are some of the additional risk-management techniques we used at Mint. They apply to any investor, large and small.

- *Use the worst-case scenario as your baseline.* I always want to know what I'm risking, and how much I can lose.
- *Only risk a very small percent of equity on any single trade.* At Mint, we never risked more than 1 percent of our total equity on any single trade. Repeat: not more than 1 percent on any single trade.

127

- *Spread your bets.* Diversify and diversify again. Make sure your diversified trades are not really more of the same kind. We traded in dozens of markets. Today you can go even wider.
- *Stick with the plan.* Like any good trading system, ours was built on sound principles and research. But if I gave it to 20 people, most of them would fail. That's because most people lack the discipline to follow the system. It is rather like people who start New Year's Day with a diet and by the middle of the month have given up.

It would be easy to stick with your trading system if it made money every single day. But no system can be right all the time and make money all the time—not a trend following system or any other system. Remember, there are four types of bets: good bets, winning bets, bad bets, losing bets. If you make good bets a thousand times, you will win—over time. How much time? We can't know. So you need to work out in advance what you will do when your system is losing money. Most people can't handle losing money. They will try to tinker, bend, or change the rules when they have a difficult time. Often it's the smartest people of all who do this—those who are most attached to their own high IQs. The last thing you want to do is find yourself in the situation where you have to meet with your partners and say, "We've been losing money for six months. What do we do?"

You will make better decisions in any kind of crisis when you are not worried about your own financial survival. The guy at the poker table who is short on chips and playing with his rent money is the guy who's going to lose. You can't make rational decisions when you are filled with fear.

You see, investors can be tragically misled by their emotions. Back in the Man years, one of my colleagues had previously been a colonel in the British Army. He was a steel-nerved individual who had specialized in dismantling bombs, the single most stressful job in the world.

I once asked him, "How did you do it?"

"It wasn't that difficult," he said. "There are different styles of bombs; a bomb in Malaysia is different from a bomb in the Middle East. You go there and see what kind of bomb it is and take it apart."

I said, "Let me ask you a question. What happens when you come across a bomb that you don't know?" He looked me in the eye and said, "You record your first impression and hope it is not your last."

I came into the office one day and found this same steel-nerved individual virtually on the brink of tears. I asked him what was wrong. It turned out that the Fed had made a major policy change, which dramatically reversed many major market trends. Overnight, our fund, which had gone from a starting value of $10 to nearly $15, had fallen back to under $12, just after he had opened a major Swiss bank as an account.

I told him, "Get them on the phone."

"What?" he asked somewhat confused. I repeated, speaking more slowly and emphatically, *"Get—them—on—the—phone."*

When I was a broker, my boss taught me that if you don't call your client when he is losing money, someone else will. And to be honest, when I was a broker, I did the same thing. When I called prospects and they complained about their broker, I would say, "Oh, how could he put you in that trade?"

So I get the account on the phone and explain that our simulations show that this type of event will occur once every few years and that I am confident that in nine months the fund will be back to a new high. "In fact," I said, "I have just borrowed some money to add to my own investment in the fund." "You really did that?" he asked in a surprised tone. I assured him I did.

Well, the account doubled up on their investment, and the fund immediately shot straight up. That account became one of Mint's biggest clients. How could I be so sure? I knew what our systems were about. What makes this business so fabulous is that, while you may not know what will happen tomorrow, you can have a very good idea what will happen over the long run.

The Mint trading system did not prioritize being right all of the time. We prioritized not losing a lot when we lost, but winning big when we won. But as a result we were frequently wrong. We understood and expected this and taught our clients the wisdom too. If you have a good system, if you have studied your odds and decided how much you are willing to lose, then stick with your system, even if the market turns against you. In our Mint days, Michael Delman liked to say that every human decision becomes an opportunity to fail. Our main success was having conceived and set this machine up so it would not depend on our judgment day-to-day and our decision-making capabilities. We all signed a written agreement that none of us could countermand the system. It was liberating to let go.

Also, tracking your volatility is a must. Volatile markets and recessions are contagions that can fool any expert. When a market is really volatile, we would stop trading and simply get out. Remember the time horizon I wrote about earlier? A speculator's advantage is choosing when to bet. Get out if the conditions are not right. Always put money on the winners.

CUTTING LOSSES AND LETTING WINNINGS RUN: THE MECHANICS OF FINDING AND FOLLOWING TRENDS

I've shared the basics of trend following in theory and how you can apply this system to love and life. It is one of the most important lessons of this book. Don't stay in bad marriages, bad jobs, or bad businesses that are failing year after year. Leave and instead seek out rising trends, then ride them for as long as they continue. Stay with the great spouse. Invest more in the business that is on the rise. Sounds great—and quite obvious when patterns are clear. But the world is full of ups and downs. How do we measure?

It's not difficult to identify stocks or commodities that are rising or falling in value. One of the most basic methods is to use "moving average," which is the average of the price of a certain asset over a given period of your choice, typically ranging from 10 days to 200 days. This is how I identify stocks or commodities that are on the move.

How do you choose your time frame? Short-term moving averages of 20 or 30 days, for example, will signal trends early, but will be more bumpy. A 200-day moving average will be slower to reflect a trend, but stronger. You set the rules as to how strong the trend is to signal a buy or sell. Action. But generally, your goal is to use moving averages that signal rising or falling trends early so you don't miss them, but long enough so the trends are real trends and not just a fleeting jolt.

I may buy stock on a rising 200-day moving average and let it run, until it starts to decline by whatever amount I've preset that I'm willing to lose, then I get out. I'm not going to sit around for a loss. I'm not there to lose money.

You can apply this principle to a range of investing scenarios. Say you can't afford to lose more than 5 percent in value of a nonretirement stock portfolio; then when you reach the 5 percent loss threshold for the portfolio overall, you can sell all the declining stocks. This is a rule that protects you against "the worst."

What percentage of your wealth are you risking? It doesn't matter how well off you are. Human beings are emotional and subject to bias when they see swings in their wealth, positive or negative. That's where we get into trouble. Letting the winners run means you don't need to sell until your stop-loss tells you to. Enjoy the ride. But don't be attached emotionally to a great investment that made you a lot of money if the market tells you to sell. By having stop-losses engrained into your money behavior, you won't make panicked or rushed decisions under pressure.

When do you want to come back to the market? When the moving average tells you that it's a good time to be there. The reverse is also true. If you're doing well and have your stop-losses in place, be careful of walking away and leaving some winnings in the universe that belong to you. Of all that I've learned as a trader and investor, letting your winnings run is the most difficult for most people.

THE BASICS OF OPTIONS AND STOPS

People believe that trading is very risky. But there is a simple device you can use to protect yourself. When you purchase a stock or commodity, you put a stop-loss order in place. This will automate a sell-off once an asset declines by an amount that you predetermined based on what you have decided you can lose.

I like to set a "trailing stop," because these adjust to trailing value, and adjustment is very important. If you buy something for $100 and you have a 2 percent stop-loss—that's $2 you're willing to lose. Once the asset goes down to $98, you're out of there. But what if the value first goes up to up to $110? With a trailing stop, you will automate your sell-off at 2 percent of $110, not $100. You stopped the loss but retained more value of what you won.

Another way of limiting your loss exposure is to buy options, something I like to do. When you buy an option (whether in commodities or the stock market), you pay a fee for the right, but not the obligation, to purchase that asset for a predetermined price during a predetermined future time period.

Why would you buy an option? Because you think you know how it's going to move. You are essentially making a *rule*. For example, say you paid $20 for a three-month option to buy a certain stock for $200 a share. Then its worth increases to $300 a share and you paid $20 for the option. You would proceed to buy and win a 50 percent profit. With the option you take two kinds of risk: price and time. Stock options are a wonderful example of asymmetrical leverage. They do not cost much, but the potential upside can be very large.

A stop-loss system isn't dramatic or exciting, but who needs drama in your money life?

DON'T PUSH YOUR LUCK WITH BAD BETS

When you learn how to cut your losses, you won't be tempted to do some of the dangerous and illegal things people do when they're in trouble with their investments. Everyone had read about the crime of insider trading, which is defined by Investopedia as "the buying or selling of a security by someone who has access to material nonpublic information about the security. Insider trading can be illegal or legal depending on when the insider makes the trade. It is illegal when the material information is still nonpublic." It's dumb: (1) You don't know if the information is good. (2) Illegal—you can go to jail.

You can always find fresh stories of people being busted on insider trading charges. To me, insider trading is one of the worst bets around and therefore has never tempted me. It's a terrible risk. First of all, you usually can't validate the sources or the information. So that's number one. Second, forget about being moral; your risk/reward has just changed dramatically because now you're going to have to go to jail. That's pure recklessness.

HOW TO LET THOSE WINNINGS RUN

When we first moved to Summit, New Jersey, we started in a modest house, but moved up and eventually wound up in an 11,000-square-foot house, where my wife Sybil and I raised our two daughters. It was a beautiful house. It was my dream. Remember, we didn't have a house when I grew up, and I grew up looking at a wall out of the window from Ocean Avenue and Avenue V. For much of my childhood I didn't even have a bedroom. This house had a heated in-ground pool, big lawns, and many rooms. My favorite was my study, which looked a lot like Don Corleone's office from *The Godfather*.

I had bought my parents an apartment in Hollywood, Florida, as I was raised to do. They had relatives there and the place was in a complex next to my rich uncle. My father wanted something simple, but I said no. All my mother's friends from Brooklyn had moved to that area, and it was good for her to be near them and be in line with their standards. Mothers have more fear than fathers, and mine lived through the Great Depression, which made her fear more acute.

After my father died, my mother came for regular visits north and stayed with us. On one of these visits, she stopped by my study after supper.

"Look, Larry, you've done well, but this is commodity trading," she said. "It's dangerous. Everyone knows that. You have enough money that you can quit."

First of all, things are not as dangerous as you think if you know what you're doing. But also, a lot of people can't deal with it if things are too good. I've noticed that this is a myth of poor people.

I looked at my mother and considered her question. "Ma," I said, "who is the richest person in our extended family?"

"Well, you, Larry."

"Do you want to keep it that way?"

"Yes, of course," she said.

"Well, what am I going to do? Go into the dress business with the other people in the family? Can you see me in that business? Mom," I continued, "I know this business. I have studied it for years and have a half dozen PhDs working for me. Wouldn't it be kind of dumb for me to get out of that business I know very well where I am an acknowledged expert, and go into the dress business because I've gotten too good at it?"

If something is too good to be true, my mother would say it probably is. I don't see it that way. I say, get smart and just enjoy it. Here's a kid who was dyslexic, blind, a poor athlete, a poor student, and now a man living in an 11,000-square-foot house. The world could turn out to be a lot better than you think.

You could say all this happened because I was a lucky *sonovabitch*. Perhaps. But I'd say it's because I had the courage to bet. And the intelligence to make smart bets. I had a goal and a plan. I had a great imagination and the idea to build a trading model that told me when to get into the markets, when to get out of the markets, and when to add more money. But mostly, I enjoy making money in the markets. There are a set criteria of facts, and I get a kick out of figuring it out or finding someone who can execute my ideas. The money is confirmation that I'm right.

I respected my mother's question, of course, and thought about it from time to time myself.

Strangely, a few weeks after this, my youngest daughter, 15 at the time and very smart, came into the Don Corleone room and said to me, "Dad, I know you're very successful and I'm very proud of you, but don't you think enough is enough?" Obviously she, too, had this fear. My wife and I both were only children. I brought my daughters up to be spoiled and protected, never to encounter abuse from anyone.

We talked awhile then, and I explained what I told her grandmother. I wasn't going to be good at anything else, I said, but more than that, simply because I am good at something doesn't mean I should stop. You let your winnings run, and that's what I was doing.

I realized I had become agnostic about wealth. The pile of money I've built is a result of a system that works in generating wealth. Its relative size isn't very important. I say that if you earned your pile through integrity and intelligence, let your winnings run. If you are generous and take care of your family, let your winnings run.

If you pay your taxes, and share what you've made with the less fortunate, let your winnings run.

There's a bad thing about being Jewish or Catholic, I've noticed: Being raised in these faiths tends to give you a sense of guilt. When things are going too well, you don't believe you are entitled. In my early years, I was not prepared to be successful. I couldn't handle it, but as time went on, I came to see that, yes, life can be better than you expect. I wish the same for you, your family, and your friends, too.

8

And the Philosophy Continues to Work: The Next Generation

After I left Mint, I managed my own money. And in 2000, I established Hite Capital, a family wealth management firm that could also serve a small roster of private clients. This let me continue my proprietary trading, and research and development in the field of systematic trading. At first, I had a goal to have no clients, as clients can become a diversion from attaining the best risk-adjusted return. Choose your clients as carefully as you choose your investments. I wanted a more stimulating and creative environment to foster new ideas. So I decided to recruit a team to help run the business—which turned out to be very smart.

I hired Alex Greyserman, who had served as director of research at Mint for over 10 years. He was responsible for research and development of trading strategies, management of Mint's assets, and overall portfolio risk management. At the time he was studying statistics at Rutgers University, where he he eventually earned a PhD. He introduced me to Reverend Thomas Bayes, an English statistician who created a mathematical for-mula for determining conditional probability. If I were to use the ace of spades in a deck of cards to illustrate the probability, that card would be 1 of 52 in the deck. If I used multiple decks, that probability changes as it does within markets. In Bayesian statistics, in a changing environment, you have to use an average. (For example, the batting average in baseball is a Bayesian statistic.) Thanks to Alex, I had a new strategy to use while assign-ing probability to any market trend.

Gilbert Lee also joined us. He was a senior research analyst for Mint and the Man Group where he imple-mented investment strategies and managed funds of over $50 million. The band was back together and we enjoyed what we were doing. We applied the same phi-losophy and system, of course, but with only this team and a few select clients who were of like mind.

THE NEXT GENERATION

My life after Mint is a good time to talk about the work of a few young people who started with me and went on to do very well. They were intelligent, willing to learn, and wanted to make money. They are close friends to this day. And they are great examples of letting your trend run with *people*.

Many excellent young people have worked for me fresh, or recently, from college. By the end of day one on the job, we'd frequently have a conversation that would begin with a statement from me along the lines of, "OK, tell me what you learned at Wharton . . . ."

Then I'd inform them that much of what they learned in school was wrong. And by this I meant all the theories and economic ideas based on the belief that markets are efficient. I told them to forget all that and would explain that I win at the markets because I know what I do not know, and that my advantage is that I am not hindered by a formal education in a quantitative field. To this day I always enjoy seeing the shock on their faces.

One such young man was Michael Levin, the son of my attorney Simon Levin. Michael went to Exeter and Wharton and interned for me in the early 1990s when he was still in college. He looked like a good bet.

In addition to the low-level work of getting coffee and lunch, he got the opportunity to do research and make stock recommendations for me. One stock he found was the Student Loan Corporation, a private bank owned largely by Citicorp that was a source of insured student loans as an intermediary for the federal government.

His research told me that demand for college loans was trending up and the Student Loan Corporation was the government's preferred intermediary. I checked his numbers, checked the trend, and put a million on it. Then I told him we'd see what happens. The stock went up 50, then 75, and 100 percent (and of course we could not predict this big move). Michael was a talented young man, so when he graduated college I offered him a job. He wanted to be an investment banker, but I told him I'd give him money to invest and a share of the profits. "If you are willing to bet on yourself, I'll bet on you."

He then worked for me from 1995 to 1999. Then he wanted to go out on his own. He had dreams that he could start the world's largest venture capital firm. As you know, I believe in dreams. I believed in Michael, so I backed his dreams and invested $5 million. The Man Group put in the same.

When I started Hite Capital Management, I let Mike and Paul Lisiak use our offices. The timing of their new venture was terrible. The tech bubble of the late 1990s burst in 1999, and all those highly overvalued tech stocks came to earth. The people at Man reacted in a way I understood, "Ok guys, thanks for trying, good effort, but no need to continue." Harsh? No, that's the *rule* in action.

They were young kids and not prepared to give up. They had accepted people's money and wanted to fulfill their promise. I said to Michael, "Why don't you come back and you can help guide and advise me on some of the Hite Capital stuff and I'll pay you and you can continue to work on these investments? I'll share 10 percent of the profits of anything you generate." I told him, here's the rule: You can do anything you want, but you have to tell me how much you will risk.

It was shaky at first. Their firm had to triage companies. But ultimately it was a worthwhile investment. By 2007, the fund we'd started in 1999 ended up delivering 350 percent of investors' capital. Today, Michael is head of asset management in Asia for Credit Suisse. He was a good bet and he never dropped low enough to hit the stop-loss I had on him, even though he hit Man's stop-loss.

But there was another element to this story that I really love: resiliency. The Man Group had allowed Michael and Paul to use their offices at the World Financial Center on the twenty-seventh floor. That was true on September 11, 2001. The horrors of that day need not be repeated here. The buildings were damaged by the attacks but not to the point of structural failure. Michael and Paul had no way to recover their documents and hard drives—there was no cloud computing or other copies. We had no idea how long the building would be closed. As young guys, they didn't have a corporate back office, nor could they afford to be out of touch with their clients. A friend of mine knew a way to get into the building. The four of us with backpacks hiked up 27 floors and loaded our haversacks with everything we could carry to salvage the documentation of their business. They were then able to set up their business in a new location.

Vikram Gokuldas is another trend following all-star I was lucky to mentor. Vikram started working for Mint as a programmer and transitioned into an analyst position. Vikram proved to me he wanted to learn and do well. Every time there was an organizational change at the office, he never complained and took on the challenge. He currently manages millions of dollars for me, which tells you how much I trust him. Are you seeing the pattern here? Good bets on people can pay off.

In much of our corporate business world, the Rule doesn't apply as easily when it comes to betting on people. Even when people are winning and making a business more successful, they can face layoffs to serve short-term goals, not the long run. When you have good people around you, give them a chance to meet and beat your expectations. Just don't expect perfection, because people aren't perfect.

Alex Greyserman was another young gun who started with me. Alex was born in the former Soviet Union and came to the United States at age 12. He had studied math, statistics, and engineering in college, then held an engineering job for a short time but had a dream of going into finance. In 1989, I was looking for a computer person to help with data and number crunching. By early 1990 he was on the job. For years, he worked for Mint crunching data as a quant. He'd spend a lot of time with me picking my brain about probability and risk. He eventually earned a promotion as director of research and then came aboard Hite Capital.

Alex taught me one of the great lessons about our trading system. He knew the secret to what we did wasn't *what* you were thinking, but *how* you were thinking. He said something early on I will never forget. He was reading some charts I gave him from our data, and after a few minutes he looked up and said, "You are running a positive mean game."

Most experts refer to this as a "positive sum game." Young investors and traders are taught Wall Street markets are a "zero-sum game" where every winner creates a loser. On the other hand, in our system, we were able to create winners.

During the Hite Capital years, Alex and I had more time for deep research. It was a wonderful opportunity. We'd been obsessed with using a large database of historical prices to run simulations of how various trend following strategies would perform over different periods of time. As I wrote in a letter to investors at the time we started Hite Capital:

Yet even after this extensive analysis, conducted by numerous PhDs both in and out of academia, no one could identify specifically how profitable any given strategy would be over any short period of time. However, what we can determine quite accurately is how much risk we are taking with each strategy, and even more so with any combination of strategies. Armed with this knowledge, we thereby know the consequences that level of risk would have gotten us in the past. So we make a more accurate prediction of the risks we are assuming.

There are many studies of trend following where researchers use data encompassing a few decades. Alex led the amazing effort to analyze data from eight centuries (yes, 800 years) of commodity and stock investing to calculate an overall rate of annualized return using trend following strategies going back to the times of those ruins I so enjoyed seeing at Angkor Wat in Cambodia.

According to Alex and Kathryn Kaminski's own recounting in *Trend Following with Managed Futures*,* we used

> monthly returns of 84 markets in equity, fixed income, foreign exchange, and commodity markets . . . as they become available from the 1200s through to 2013. . . . A representative trend following system represents the performance of "following the trend" throughout the centuries in whatever markets might be available. . . .

---

* Alex Greyserman and Kathryn Kaminski, *Trend Following with Managed Futures: The Search for Crisis Alpha*, Wiley, 2013.

At any point in time, to calculate whether a trend exists, the portfolio consists of only markets that have had at least a 12-month history.

Wow. We looked at 84 markets over 800 years with a minimum data threshold of a year's performance. And we showed that over the 800-year period, representative trend following strategies generated an annual return of *13 percent*, with an annualized volatility of 11 percent. This far outperformed the comparison buy-and-hold strategy that delivered 4.8 percent.

Our study confirmed (yet one more time) our understanding of human nature. Human beings like to create booms and bubbles, which is predictable even if we don't know the exact timing of the next big event. Look, I could have made a fortune during the Holland tulip boom, as our study demonstrated a trend follower would have made handsome profits exiting the tulip market far ahead of the crash. Take Black Monday (1987) and the Crash of 1929. The study showed a trend following strategy would have delivered a 90 percent return between October 1928 and October 1930!

As I wrote earlier, Michael Covel has confirmed similar findings in his landmark book—trend following really can shine during tough market times. Here's something else that our study proved: "Black swans"—those supposedly surprise events that cause market chaos—have always been with us. As Alex and Kathryn summarized,

"The positive performance of trend following during crisis periods is not specific to the 1929 Wall Street crash, the performance during the Dutch Tulip mania. In fact, the strategy seems to perform well during the most difficult periods in history."

In another simulation project at the time, we wanted to ascertain the value of "perfect knowledge." So we came up with another model. Quoting my letter again,

> What if we knew the ending prices at the end of the year across a portfolio of markets? In an attempt to answer our own question, we went to our databases and looked up the prices on December 31 of a given year and then asked ourselves, "With this knowledge, how much leverage could we have used to get the maximum advantage at the beginning of that same year on January 1?" We found that even with perfect foresight of the ending price we could not sustain more than 3 to 1 leverage, because we could not predict the path it took to get there.
>
> Counterintuitively, one conclusion that we have reached is that leverage can be used to decrease risk by having multiple strategies in uncorrelated assets. We can materially reduce the standard deviation of our portfolio and thereby lower our risk.

Life proves again and again that even the most rigorous efforts to predict market behavior will be foiled by human ambition and our desire to believe a good story when it is more appealing than a solid fact.

WHAT'S IN A NAME?
HOW 25 DOLLARS BECAME TWO MILLION

Alex and Michael helped pull off one of the great asymmetrical leverage moves of my career. In 1994, Alex suggested we buy the domain name mint.com, which was available. So we did and we all had mint.com email addresses. That was all well and good; no one thought too much about it. The domain name market had not developed the way it has today.

Then in 2006 Aaron Patzer contacted us. Patzer was launching an online financial services tool through his company Mint Software, Inc. He needed the mint.com URL. Patzer spoke to Alex and offered $100,000. We all thought that wasn't going to change our lifestyles in a dramatic way, but we were intrigued. Michael checked out Mint Software and relayed they had a ton of high-grade venture capital, a strong business plan, and vision for the future. We thought they could be pretty special and we should look at getting equity.

I contacted Patzer's people and said we won't sell it for money, only for equity. They resisted. Well, I told them we didn't need $100,000, so they can find another URL. Patzer relented and gave us 2 percent of the company, including anti-dilution rights so we would maintain our stake when the company expanded their capital.

In 2009, Patzer sold the company to Intuit for $177 million. That made our share $4 million for an investment that was less than a few hundred dollars when Alex bought the domain name in the early 1990s. Michael and Alex also put in a little money and got a nice cut as well. I donated my share to one of the Hite charities. Now *that* was cool!

A RETURN TO MANAGING OTHER PEOPLE'S MONEY

Alex and Gilbert came with me in 2010 when I joined a new fund venture to work with my friend from ED&F Man, Lord Stanley Fink. Lord Fink was recovering from surgery and a health scare and wanted to get back to work on a new venture. He'd left Man and wanted to build up a new fund with the kind of trading we did at Mint. As the *Financial Times* reported on February 21, 2010,

> the systematic strategy used by AHL, Man Group's powerhouse fund, was pioneered by Mr. Hite in the 1980s and 1990s in the United States, and it was under Mr. Fink's leadership at Man that it reached its peak. Mr. Hite's development of complex, algorithmically driven models that aimed to spot and follow

market trends delivered average annualized returns of more than 30 percent to his clients.

Hite Capital was merged into a flagship fund, called International Standard Asset Management (ISAM). ISAM started with about $700 million under management. Our purpose was to run trend following strategies in 250 different types of markets for outside clients guided by the same philosophy and principles.

Lord Fink wanted to get back in the quantitative game and didn't have a system equal to what we'd done with Hite Capital. Stanley told us the strength of what we did was in the depth of our historical testing and capabilities of our risk management in volatile markets. He set up the corporation and we were back in the big game. Again, don't fight the opportunity. When one arrives—jump on.

If I liked working on my own projects, you might want to know, why did I go back to work at ISAM? I wanted to do this with and for Stanley, but I was particularly gratified that Alex would become a partner in the firm as chief scientist. He was one of my earliest bets, and seeing him ride his personal trend was exciting for me.

Then there's a second, more interesting answer. Many years ago, I had a client, a gentleman in the baked goods industry. He came to me after selling his business for $10 million. In discussing his options, I explained that this kind of thing doesn't happen very often. He quickly corrected me. He had done this very type of deal several times. He explained he had a simple formula for success. First, he kept to an industry he knew very well, which was bakeries, and he only partnered with men in their mid-30s. They were young enough to have energy and youth, but old enough to be tempered by experience.

I could immediately see the beauty of this fellow's philosophy and kept it in mind when considering new ventures of my own.

Lord Fink served as chairman until stepping down from ISAM in December 2018. I enjoyed those early years at ISAM. However, I would rather be an investor like Warren Buffett, pick the one stock that's going to do well and go off and do public speaking and conferences, but I could never live with that volatility. As Alex will say, "ISAM was the most boring place in the world. Nobody yelled. Nobody panicked or screamed over their phones. You entered the trades, the money came out, and it got sent away." Alex is chief scientist and one of the key players within the company.

IDENTIFY THE WORST THING THAT CAN HAPPEN IN ANY SCENARIO

You may be thinking, a lot of bad things happened in these years. What about market crashes caused by acts of terrorism, or real estate economic bubbles that crashed Wall Street's trading algorithms and resulted in spiraling losses? I have seen many crises in my life such as the 2008 crash and global recession but certainly September 11 was a catastrophic event like no other. As devastating as such events were for people around the world, bad things happen throughout history and you don't want to lose all your money when they do.

Yet, knowing the worst possible outcome gives you tremendous freedom.

Some fund managers will say the worst that can happen financially is going broke and losing your clients' principal. We learned in 2008 and with Madoff that actually there are worse outcomes. Some investors skirt or break the laws or become hopelessly corrupt and when this happens, they tend to get caught.

You want to identify the worst thing that can happen in any scenario and plan for it. I once gave a speech to an audience of people who had only recently become millionaires. The subject was "preserving wealth in the face of market volatility." These people knew they were rich at the time, but didn't know if they were still going to be rich in 10 years.

I walked out on stage carrying a properly furled black British umbrella.

I opened the umbrella and closed it a few times, maintaining eye contact with the audience. They were confused, but I had their attention. Then I told them about the time I was visiting London to attend my mother-in-law's funeral. I decided on the morning after the ceremony to take a walk on Hampstead Heath, near my wife's family home. The weather was bright and beautiful, but my wife advised me, "Take an umbrella."

I told her, "Are you trying to tell me to take an umbrella when I have been traveling to London one week out of six over the past seven years?"

She said, "Are you trying to tell me you know more than me about London weather? I lived here for 26 years!"

I left the umbrella at home and took my walk on the Heath. Not only did it rain, it poured and then the rain turned to hail. I was soaked like a dog after a cold bath.

So again, I peer out at the tittering group from my place on the stage. "The best time to think about risk is before you start," I said, and they laughed hard.

A friend of mine who is very wealthy said if you never bet your lifestyle, from a trading standpoint, nothing bad will ever happen to you, and if you know what the worst possible outcome is from the outset, you will have tremendous freedom. My rules of thumb for a crisis are no different than our historic approach to risk management:

- Use the worst-case scenario as your baseline. I always want to know what I'm risking, and how much I can lose.
- Be prepared to lose capital that is subject to market volatility. You alone control how much of your limited supply of money you are willing to lose. Never expose more of your pile to volatility than you can afford.

- Be prepared to lose roughly the size of your annual return. For example, a strategy with a 10 percent return over time should be expected to suffer at least double the annual return in a 20 percent drawdown—so a strategy with a 30 percent return over time should be expected to suffer a 60 percent drawdown.

Finally, isn't it true that you make better decisions in any kind of crisis when you are not worried about your own financial survival and the terrible pressures of those feelings? You can't make rational decisions when you have an unhealthy fear of the risks involved.

Always, always identify the worst that can happen and change your behavior to protect yourself and maybe your family.

9

Conversations with a Young Trader— with Kolade Oluwole

A major purpose of this book is to teach other people about how I was successful as a trader and how those insights apply to their own circumstances. I also enjoy talking with young traders I meet in my travels, as another form of teaching. And Kolade's (Kahla-day) story is one I really like. The American-born son of a Nigerian father and American mother, Kolade studied engineering in college but harbored a growing passion for trading and learning to invest. He reminded me of my long-standing colleague Alex Greyserman, another engineer who came to me wanting to learn about getting into the markets. Then I had an idea: Let's meet and have a talk and share it *Market Wizards* style. So we set it up. Kolade, in his early twenties—just out of college—and I, in my seventies, enjoyed a valuable and informal dialogue about how to make a mint in quantitative trading. Now that you've read a major portion of the book, this discussion offers a way of hearing the principles being discussed "live."

KOLADE: Larry, I really appreciate the opportunity to talk to you—to talk to someone with a lot of experience. I initially wanted to get into futures to trade Bitcoin. I could see that I could short the market and make profits as the price of Bitcoin decreases. I have been trading for some months now mostly in Bitcoin futures and other derivatives. All these pieces are relatively similar in the way they pay. I am just going to jump in with an opening question.

LARRY: Sure.

KOLADE: The markets are volatile. They are hard to predict. I understand that traders can and will be wrong some of the time. They need to limit their losses and watch their leverage. My question is: How do you go about creating a system and how do you really build an edge in trading?

LARRY: My complete edge is that before I do anything, I know exactly how much I am betting. I know exactly why I am betting it. I know exactly when I am going to get out of that bet. I am a trend follower. It has kept me alive and made me pretty wealthy. I look at an opportunity to break out, I buy it. But the moment I buy it, I have a stop in mind.

KOLADE: Even if you have complete knowledge, you don't have complete knowledge of how prices will unfold. I mean, do you have any complete knowledge?

LARRY: I've been doing this for 40 years. I made money as a venture capitalist. I made a lot of money trading commodities. For that span of time, I have always started with how much I am willing to lose.

KOLADE: How much *are* you willing to lose?

LARRY: I am willing to lose a percentage, maybe 2 percent on a trade. I am an across-the-board trend follower. I don't even look at whatever fundamental demand is, it doesn't matter to me—to be blunt.

KOLADE: Could you address how trend following plays out in a specific trading activity, whether it's futures, whether it's the stock market? Your edge is trend following. Explain more.

LARRY: I get on and off trends, based on price averaging in various time intervals, 10 days, 100 days, 200 days—whatever the rule I decide. If a price goes above that average, you become a buyer. If a price dips below that average, you become a seller.

The difference between what you are buying at and what you sell at is what you are risking of your core capital. Your core capital is what you got; that is your pool of trading dollars. You are not going to overtrade it, if you understand what I am saying.

KOLADE: I do. Overtrading can be a real problem. I actually have a question about the number of trades in general. When you are really actively trading in the market, how many trades do you make in a year or in a week?

LARRY: I will go across the board without really knowing the exact number in advance. Whichever hits on my criteria, which gives me a break out or break down and will lose me no more than 2 percent of my capital on that trade—those are my trades.

KOLADE: That's it?

LARRY: Sort of like a little dance, right? You go to a high school dance and there are many girls there. Some you might like more than others. So you go up to find a girl to talk to. You get rebuffed or a girl might agree to dance with you.

KOLADE: Yep.

LARRY: You might go up to a girl, and something just doesn't work. What do you do? You look for somebody else.

KOLADE: All right, so how do you identify the attractive girls when it comes to trading?

LARRY: Are they making a new high? That tells you the trend is up. Or if you hit a six-month low or one-month low, that is your stop. The market has to show me. I'm not telling the market. If the market shows me which way it is going, I'll jump on the train. So if one girl turns me down, I say thank you very much, and I go to the next girl and ask her for a dance. We dance a bit and have a good time, maybe we go to dinner, and then we have a big trend.

KOLADE: If you are at the dance, what's a good time to go ask that girl to dance? You probably don't want to ask her when she is talking to two other guys. When do you jump on a trend? When do you see that opportunity?

LARRY: When the price makes a new high and you are there and can participate. When the market does something that shows me which direction it is going. If it jumps up over the six-month average, that is an indicator. That shows me which way the market is going. That's the time. If you buy nothing but new highs in whatever market, then you must have a stop. The important thing is the stop. The stop keeps you alive. That's it. Do you know who David Ricardo was?

KOLADE: No I don't.

LARRY: David Ricardo was one of the major, major financiers in the 1700s. He became one of the richest men in England. As a hobby he and a couple of guys happen to have invented market economics. But he loved the markets for trading, too. He used to say, when you go in and buy a stock, and it is winning, let your profits run. People get rich when they let their profits run. You just don't know how far the run will go, so don't get out early.

You are looking for those huge profits, and you want to get as much as you can without making the risk more than 8 percent of your capital.

KOLADE: Can the market ever get too high?

LARRY: Look at what has happened with life expectancy. Now people are living well into their eighties and nineties all over the place. People are much healthier. So who knows? A good way to keep yourself grounded—you look at the cash flow versus the price. Kolade, here's a question for you: Are you an investor or are you a trader?

KOLADE: I am a trader by far.

LARRY: Why? Warren Buffett is not a trader. He buys companies he thinks will give him strong cash flow going out 10, 20 years. Many of these companies are undervalued in the eyes of the markets, so he is doing a version of buy low and sell high. There are a number of sound models for building wealth.

KOLADE: Yeah. He looks at the fundamentals and he invests. I like to look at what the trend tells me, whether the trend is double tops, double downs, triangles, I look where the trend is trading, where it is going, and I want to trade based on that.

I don't want to invest and hold for 20 years. I like to go in while it's hot, ride it, then when it turns against me, I get out. I read a lot about trend following before talking to you, and it made sense to me because when you are in a good trade, you can just let it go. It keeps growing and growing and growing until it turns against you and you get out. Warren Buffett will hold a trade for 20 years.

LARRY: It also made him one of the richest men in the world. Every serious person I've known who followed Buffett's example did get rich. But I prefer trend following. I believe one of the strongest things man has is the gene for adaptability. The markets give you a chance to adapt.

It's like running a casino to me. If you are running a casino, you know certain people are going to beat the casino. Out of a hundred people, five might have the lucky night or be expert poker players. They beat the casino. But on balance, the casino has all the numbers on its side. The casino knows how to count, so it will always win overall. But if you want to win at your particular angle on a particular night, you have to find what out what is happening at the game, you have to know the odds and play the odds. And you may have to go against your own personality.

Certainly, if I said to you, buy a stock at five times earnings, let's say over the next 20 years. And you can keep pyramiding and you can make a billion dollars with one stock. Would you do that?

KOLADE: I would do that.

LARRY: You never escape what you are and who you are. You have a certain temperament; now at a certain age, you like double tops in trading. You might very well become interested in real estate at a later point in your life. Whatever your money goal, trend following is an arbitrage of the cost of money versus what you want. The other thing is to help you decide: You need a goal. Do you know how to define *rich*?

KOLADE: I think *rich* is relative, and I would define my rich as financially free.

LARRY: That's a good thing. How much money do you need to be financially free?

KOLADE: More than I have now and less than you have now.

LARRY: Give me an amount you think you could make in trading that would make you say, yeah, I'm rich now.

KOLADE: If I had a number?

LARRY: Yes. How old are you?

KOLADE: I'm 23.

LARRY: At 33, how wealthy do you want to be?

KOLADE: At 33, I want to have a couple million dollars in assets. I really don't care about the dollars in my bank account, but at least create accounts in real estate, and at least work in a good business, make good connections. I think it's important to have your dollars in your bank as a stable foundation.

LARRY: You have to pick a very specific amount.

KOLADE: Very specific?

LARRY: If you have goals, they are an incredibly powerful thing. You should pick some people who you think have the kind of life you want. And it doesn't matter if you know them or have spoken to them. Just what do you want? What are you going to do with it? You have to actually define rich. Robert Kiyosaki defines rich this way—if you can live for 3 years on just the cash that you have. In 10 years, what do you think that 3-year number would be? For 5 years? Or 2 years? You have to know what you are aiming for.

KOLADE: I remember that chapter. I read his book.

LARRY: There used to be a company called ITT. It was run by a big-time guy named Harold Geneen. Harold took a shine to me. He took me to lunch one day and said, "Larry, do you like movies?" Of course, I answered. Then he told me a lesson he would often repeat to me when we saw each other. When you go the movies, you don't know how it will end, and that suspense keeps you engaged. When you buy a business, you better know the ending already. You better know exactly what you are going to do with it and how you are going to do it before you buy it. That's a difference between going to the movies and buying a business. This is also the difference between the conventional buy-and-hold strategy and trend following. We always know when we'll get out and why. We know how the trade will end up at the opening credits.

KOLADE: Cool.

LARRY: Kolade, do you program? It can really help on my style of trading.

KOLADE: I know a little bit. I have done some C and some Java, some CFF, HTML.

LARRY: The great thing about my style of investing is it's been done before, and you can use your coding ability to look back in time and test trading rules against older data. You can see when a strategy works or doesn't work. You see, the great thing about investing is you don't have to invest.

KOLADE: What do you mean?

LARRY: Unless you know enough about a trade, you don't do it. You have to know how you are going to do it, why you are doing it, the way you do it, how long you are going to do it, and you have to plan that out. It takes practice to develop that discipline, and you can do that by buying a database to do simulated trading and get some practice. Use simulations to test your ability to understand where the numbers are going.

KOLADE: OK.

LARRY: If you build simulations, you're seeing mathematical evidence, probabilities, odds, risks. There is no wishy-washy in there. I like numbers because they're not open to interpretation. They're facts. If I am sitting in Miami and I say to you the sea is blue, what does that mean? Was I talking about dark blue, light blue, royal blue, powder blue? When I say seven, you know it's seven. Not only do you know seven, people will look at the same seven and they will know it's seven. You want to be very definite in what and how and when and why you are doing something.

KOLADE: You are saying that running simulations is well worth the time, as a process of thinking through goals and how you get to them?

LARRY: Yes. All of that. You want to simulate. So go and practice. It costs you nothing to practice.

KOLADE: I agree.

LARRY: Start with options, for example. You can define exactly how to use them. You know precisely what you are going to get. Don't get confused with whether you are buying currencies or selling Bitcoin. What you're trading doesn't matter. What matters is the single fundamental constant in markets. You know what that is?

KOLADE: No. What is it?

LARRY: The biggest fundamental in the markets are people. That's it. People. People have not changed in thousands of years.

KOLADE: How long did it take you to learn this game? How long did it take you to become a really profitable trader? To understand that you are trading risks and get your edge? How long was your journey?

LARRY: The journey was to get rich. Once I knew how to do it, I followed my own plan. I met a lot of people who got lost in their journey because they could not take a loss. I had a conversation with a relative of mine who actually was a good trader, but he couldn't call a loss a loss. He was afraid to cut his losses. He wound up bankrupt. It's not that it's hard to cut your losses and let your winnings run. But the actual doing it for some is very hard. For other people, it comes naturally, and I suppose I was one of them. That's the nature of my journey. An exact time to get there? Can't give you that.

KOLADE: I imagine if I talk to a hundred traders, none of them would say, "I really like to let my losses run." How is the David Ricardo, Larry Hite vision of cutting your losses different from what, say, I might hear from a lot of other experts? No one is going to say, "Yeah losses are great. Let them run. I want more and bigger losses."

LARRY: What are they doing about cutting their losses? *That is the issue.*

KOLADE: Why do we have this behavior that interferes with the good way?

LARRY: It all starts with you. You must know what risks you will take. You must have a fair idea of what you can afford to lose. You must know approximately what you should get. You must be very detached from what you are trading. Some people are just the opposite. They really think they know *everything* and believe they do. I have had competitors who were utterly confident they were the smartest people in the world. *But they forgot the most important thing is to stay alive.* They took on too much risk, and a huge loss swamped their many small wins. Look, what I do is called a positive mean game. I keep my losses small and when I win, I win on a large scale so I am never in danger of having a negative mean.

If you treat trading like a game, because that is what it is, then you will find there are a lot of variations in trading, but a good process will work over time and you will get rich if you stick with it.

KOLADE: That sounds good to me.

LARRY: I think you got a good mathematical mind to understand it. It's a perseverance game. If you start with the losses you can handle, you will get richer. Back when my mother lived in Brooklyn, I would come home once a week. She'd ask me, "How did you do?" I'd say, "You know, I lost $100,000." She would go, "Oh God, that's terrible!" But she couldn't understand that to me it wasn't a big deal, because it was a very, very tiny percentage of our fund (less than 2 percent, typically). I mean, if you have $100 in your pocket and you lose a single dollar, will you really be upset?

KOLADE: No.

LARRY: She saw the amount of money. I saw the percentage.

KOLADE: You just naturally have that gift to not really care about how much it was, but care about the percent. You know most people would not be able to take a loss like this.

LARRY: I had an advantage. I was a terrible athlete. I was used to losing. If you lose, you figure out how to keep your losses small and your winnings big. It's that ratio. How much are you willing to bet out of your deck? It's a mindset. Are there people who do it differently? Yes.

Some of them might do well, maybe find some great luck, but I find the majority of people who do well are in large part trend followers. When I started in this business, not too many of us were doing this. I encourage you to develop this mindset. I think you can get it. If you keep your losses small as you go along, you got it. Now, you might wind up working for a firm, but one of the reasons I stopped working for a firm is that they have politics, committees, and gossip. I wasn't interested in any of that. My addiction in getting into this is to have my own money. I didn't want to work for anybody. I didn't want to be really good at meetings.

I wanted to be really good at trading. I wanted to be rich.

KOLADE: Financial freedom.

LARRY: Decide if you're going to be a good hunter or a good BS'er. When the survival of the tribe depended upon having good hunts, the best hunters weren't hanging around when the bison were running. They weren't in the lodge talking about who had the sharpest spear or could throw it the farthest. The more good hunters a tribe had, the more of them who survived. Today, great traders set the odds like they're owning a casino. The edge piles up over time. You know winners because they won. The capital is going up. You are doing something right.

KOLADE: Thanks, Larry!

10

You Have Choices: Persistence Pays Dividends

often think back about my childhood and youth and remember what a failure I was—poor, half-blind, dyslexic, uncoordinated, unathletic—and the least likely to succeed. Yet I beat the odds. It wasn't until I was well into my thirties that things started happening, but up until that point no one saw my potential. No one could have predicted my path.

If I'd had an easier path, I doubt I'd have been as successful as I was. That's because failure was the foundation of my success. People talk about the power of positive thinking, but I found power in negative thinking. Losing was normal, and I was intimately acquainted with it. I had lost so much that I had nothing to lose, so losing couldn't crush me. I just kept getting up and trying again. That's the real secret of winning.

Larry's Tips for Getting Back on Your Feet When Life Happens

1. Don't hide your losses; get them in the open.
2. Get smart people to help you by cutting them in on the profits.
3. Keep human emotion away from the equation.
4. Have a scheme.
5. Be open to a fresh start and working farther from home.
6. Never be impulsive with your career.
7. Make it easy for people to work with you.

• • •

Why did someone who failed at so many things for so long, do well?

From the very beginning I was looking at the probability of where I could be successful in life. I immediately ruled out all the things I couldn't do well. I never would have been a great athlete. I was never going to cure my dyslexia and become a great scholar. Those odds were just too long. Once I ruled out the bad bets, I could go and do other things to get to the goal.

In the good bets department, I chose to do something that I loved so much I would have done it for free. When you make this choice, you will give yourself a tremendous edge, too, because you will work harder at it than most other people. I loved inventing ways to earn money. I spend time on the phone for hours working on it. For me it is fun.

And of course, as you know I had the power of want: I really had a sincere desire to have economic freedom.

I have shared my personal stories of failure and success along the way to show that your dreams can overcome your limitations. I hope you see that things can turn out better than you expect and that you can beat the odds.

Like most people, I was taught the value of hard work. But it quickly became clear to me that hard work is overrated. Smart work pays infinitely more. The business executive conducting a multimillion dollar deal at a restaurant is not working harder than the lowest-paid worker washing dishes in the kitchen. But the executive is wealthier. Naturally, these roles can be reversed if the dishwasher begins working smarter and training for a higher-paying job and the executive is fired for cheating on her expense reports.

Everyone has choices to make. Whether you are a trader, a songwriter, or a dishwasher, your choices define your humanity and your life. You have the power to get out of a bad marriage or a bad job. You have the power to go through school. You have the power to not be 300 pounds. If you have a dream, make the choice to do something each day to advance your cause.

The problem is that people don't think enough about choices in terms of probability. But this is how you make smart bets. And if you make enough smart bets, you will win.

The next time you are making a choice about your path for life, a business venture, or your investment portfolio, ask yourself these questions:

- *Which choice brings you closer to your goal?* Let your imagination go a few steps ahead. This is why I encourage you to know yourself and what you want. So many people are sold on the value of a great education. I believe profoundly in education. But if you don't know yourself and what you want, it will do you no good.
- *Are you playing the game in the right place?* A lot of wealth is generated by luck, but you've got to be in a place where you could get lucky. If you want to be an actor but you don't audition, you can't win. I remember a young actor I knew who was so stiff and awkward that he was the least likely to succeed. But he was in the right place and got his break. He grew to become an excellent actor and eventually made it on Broadway. You've got to have butterfly wings.
- *Is your choice doable?* If you made this bet a thousand times, what would the odds be? Remember, I wasn't going to be Michael Jordan or Lebron James. It

simply wasn't doable. But being a trader was possible because of my natural abilities, persistence, and how much I loved it. Even so, I had no formal mathematics training or computer skills. So I partnered with people who brought those skills to the table. Then my goals became doable. What is doable for you?

- *What is the worst thing that can happen?* Look the worst thing straight in the eye before you decide to bet. You have to know what you can lose. If you can't afford the worst thing that can happen, then it's a bad bet.

- *If you win it, what do you get?* This is the money question. It's the payoff that will give you the best expected value of what you want. So ask yourself what's the payoff? Is it a small amount or big enough to make a difference? If you make a bet that wins you a dollar a year, is that really winning? I made money because I found an asymmetrical bet. I could risk little and win a lot. In finance, you can use options and stops to do this. Or in life, you can use your knowledge, time, and the investment of other people in a partnership. Go to places where you can make multiples of what you are risking.

- *After you make your choice, will you have the humility to change if it isn't working?* Failure is merely a singular event. It doesn't mean you are a failure as a person. If you fail, cut your losses and stop doing what is losing. Get out of there and find the next good bet as quickly and intelligently as you can.

• • •

Some people might say, "Well, Larry, you were *lucky*. You arrived on the scene at the moment when commodities and computerized models were just taking off." There may be some truth to that. But the world of finance still offers people opportunity, perhaps even more opportunity than when I was young. We are in a technology revolution. Computers used to be the size of refrigerators, and now they are the size of a credit card, and they are getting cheaper and cheaper. Next will be advanced robots and sensors and artificial intelligence. We will have self-driving cars soon enough.

Markets are inefficient, as I have said many times in this book. It is precisely in their inefficiency that they offer opportunity. If markets were efficient, people would have no incentive to work or invent. Their inefficiency creates incentives for people to innovate and create better, faster, cheaper services and products. That means there is always something on the table for people to work harder at, pursue, and achieve. Over time, as certain innovations become the new normal, then the edge wears away. But that means new opportunities arise for new markets. It is your job to find those opportunities in your own time and place. I assure you they are *there*. All you have to do is understand what you want. What are the traits you want? You don't know the thing but you know what you want it to look like.

WHAT HAPPENS WHEN YOU WIN?

While you are on the way to making your fortune, you should plan for what you will do when you win.

I don't really care about luxuries, although I live very well. My thing is creativity. In my eighth decade, I am still motivated by inventing new ways to make money. I am just as interested as ever in the next innovation. I call up my quant partner and ask him to test ideas, like, "What happens if we randomly choose a stock that reaches an all-time high?"

In recent years, I've started to buy real estate. In my usual fashion, I've found smart people to work with who have expertise that I don't. Here was their equation. They buy buildings where they figure they can buy it with full or near full occupancy and rent it at 10 percent less than the market. They do what they have to do to make it comparable to a better building, but they rent 10 percent less. This is brilliant because they keep occupancy. What they do is five to seven years later, they remortgage—"mortgaging out." In other words, they reborrow. But now they have cash. It's almost like they sold the building, except they don't have to pay tax on it. Instead, they borrowed the money, and they still have the building. With the cash from Building 1, they buy Building 2. If you borrow the money, you pay no tax. They take depreciation in certain parts. Certain parts of the building wear out faster. So we do the accounting based on accelerating depreciation.

People who are doing real estate this way get very rich. They don't have the best buildings. They're not Trump, who piles on the elegance and luxury on the lower floors but cuts back on the upper floors where the rooms are smaller and have less appeal. They are making the best deal. And I am making a lot of money this way, too.

That's what I do. It's my same process over and over, but with new opportunities.

• • •

I started my foundation in 1987. I was on a winter vacation in the Caribbean and made a phone call to execute a trade. That single call made me a million dollars. What a great feeling. The following week, when I got back to New York, I was walking through the World Trade Center late one evening and saw large numbers of people entering. Many of them looked like they were not in the best condition. I asked the security people what was going on, and they explained that it was going to be freezing that night and homeless people were coming inside to sleep. Now my feeling had changed. The million dollars felt not so important. That was when I really started to think about how I could help.

Someone once asked me if I give away money because I feel guilty. I do not feel guilty. And I do not give because I am a religious man. But I do seek to live by the golden rule, which seems to be the one idea that most everyone agrees to, at least on paper. Confucius described it in a way that I particularly like: When asked if there was one word that could serve as a principle of conduct for life, he replied, "It is the word *shu*—reciprocity. Do not impose on others what you yourself do not desire."

I believe in reciprocity.

The first time I made a major donation was for a young lady in Azerbaijan who needed an operation. She had doctors and a hospital that were willing to give her the operation for free in San Francisco, but she and her mother had to get there. The cost was $10,000, so I eagerly made that happen. That was my gift. I was happy to save a life. But I'm a practical person, so over time, I began to think about how I could make the biggest impact, rather than for just one person.

In 1987, I started a family foundation so I could give in a smart way and make the biggest impact on as many lives as possible. At first, the foundation was relatively small and we met payout requirements by giving to our favorite charities. But as I became more successful and gave more, the foundation grew larger, and we hired a consultant so we could be strategic and professional about it. When our daughters became juniors in high school, they had a chance to get involved and (with supervision) make a $5,000 grant to an organization of their choice. Our older daughter gave to an afterschool program in Newark, New Jersey, and our younger daughter gave to a photography program for children at a museum. (Interestingly, one daughter became a therapist and the other a historian of photography.)

We have given to many different kinds of causes. My first wife, Sybil, had a master's degree in social work and had spent 10 years working with children in the NYC foster care system. She believed that all kids should have safe, loving homes, so our foundation funded organizations that reformed the foster care system. She also loved photography and art, so we funded exhibitions at the major museums in New York City and in Britain.

Again, I'm a practical person. When I invest I want the greatest return, and when I give, I want to impact the most people. That's one reason why I give to medical research. Who knows? Maybe in 20 years one of organizations I am funding will find the cure for cancer.

My friend Stanley Fink has a similar perspective. In 2005, he donated money for a new building for Evelina London, the first new children's hospital in London in a hundred years. Not long after that, my wife Sybil was dying. She was from London, and another friend from the Man Group, Harvey McGrath, had a wife, Allison. I told Harvey that my wife missed knowing about London gossip, and I asked if Allison would be so kind as to give her a call and gossip about London society once a week? Allison did exactly this, and I will never forget it. When I donated six preemie beds to the neonatal unit at Evelina, I made the gift in honor of Sybil Hite and Allison McGrath.

Since then, probably a thousand kids have used those cribs. I don't know them or how their lives turned out. But I know that I helped do something to improve their odds. How many times do you get a chance to do something that helps a thousand people?

Some years ago, I also became interested in freeing scholars who are repressed by totalitarian governments. Usually scholars and intellectuals are the first to speak out against dictators, and they are likely to get put in jail or killed. Henry Kaufman and Allan Goodman are good people trying to save lives, very special people who lead the Scholar Rescue Fund. Through them I learned about a PhD biologist who was doing medical research in Uganda. During the revolution a soldier came up to him and said he wanted his truck. The researcher said no because he had to bring it to an experiment. Finally the soldier took out a gun and blew out his brains. The researcher was one of five PhDs in Uganda. One bullet destroyed so much in that nation.

I got to thinking that this guy's medical research could have saved a thousand people's lives. So I put the question to myself yet again: How many times do I get a chance to save a thousand people? So I supported the Scholar Rescue Fund that helps gets persecuted scholars out of their oppressive countries by giving them fellowships at universities where they can live safely and do their work. What I learned from my training is this: The best thing that can happen is that I save someone whose work might save many lives. The worst thing that can happen is that I can save one life. Both are good bets.

In recent years, my current wife, Sharon, and I have given to organizations that promote education and culture. We donate to musical organizations because it seems to me that music is one of the greatest gifts we experience from being alive.

I am grateful for the choices I made in my life that put me now in the unique position of being able to create stuff that continues to make money and might make the world better. I wish the same for you.

• • •

If—

Rudyard Kipling

If you can keep your head when all about you
    Are losing theirs and blaming it on you,
If you can trust yourself when all men doubt you,
    But make allowance for their doubting too;
If you can wait and not be tired by waiting,
    Or being lied about, don't deal in lies,
Or being hated, don't give way to hating,
    And yet don't look too good, nor talk too wise:

If you can dream—and not make dreams your master;
    If you can think—and not make thoughts your aim;
If you can meet with Triumph and Disaster
    And treat those two impostors just the same;
If you can bear to hear the truth you've spoken
    Twisted by knaves to make a trap for fools,
Or watch the things you gave your life to, broken,
    And stoop and build 'em up with worn-out tools:

If you can make one heap of all your winnings
    And risk it on one turn of pitch and-toss,
And lose, and start again at your beginnings
    And never breathe a word about your loss;
If you can force your heart and nerve and sinew
    To serve your turn long after they are gone,
And so hold on when there is nothing in you
    Except the Will which says to them: "Hold on!"

If you can talk with crowds and keep your virtue,
    Or walk with Kings—nor lose the common touch,
If neither foes nor loving friends can hurt you,
    If all men count with you, but none too much;
If you can fill the unforgiving minute
    With sixty seconds' worth of distance run,
Yours is the Earth and everything that's in it,
    And—which is more—you'll be a Man, my son!

I think much of what I've said over these pages is summed up by this poem by Rudyard Kipling. (With apologies for the last line speaking to men. Kipling was a man of his time, and I am a man of mine and believe the poem applies to women equally as well.)

Some of us are up against tougher odds from the start. But the core of my message is this: Your dreams are bigger than your limitations, and you can make a choice to follow them.

Regardless of your circumstances you have choice. I want my grandchildren to grow up knowing they have choices. And I won't feel that this book is successful unless you come away feeling you can make choices that will change your life too.

My trading is based on speculation. But my life itself is also a speculator's game. Inherently we cannot know what will happen. There are many "ifs." We are constantly buying into things and getting out of them. Our choices of what to buy into and what to get out of are ultimately how we create our lives and ultimately how we create meaning.

My life is proof that a loser can win.

—APPENDIX—

Pieces of Mind

The Theory and Practice of Asymmetrical Leverage (Arranging Big Wins for Small Risks), Larry Hite, internal paper written for EDF Man.

The Theory and Practice
of Asymmetrical Leverage
(Arranging Big Wins for Small Risks)

September 30, 1988

PREFACE

The purpose of this paper is to state clearly the principles of Asymmetrical Leverage (AL). Since these are theoretical rather than quantitative concepts, they cannot be tested on a computer in the way that the MIMC strategies were. The only viable test is to have them debated and considered against a wide range of first class business experience. That is the reason you have been chosen to read this paper.

In a nutshell, I would rather have my colleagues point out the flaws in my reasoning than have the marketplace teach them to me.

DEFINITION

AL is unique in that it affords one the benefits of conventional leverage minus the proportional risk. To cite an example, MIMC currently has an arrangement with a Middle Eastern institution for whom we constructed a $15 million Islamic portfolio where, after the agent's fees, we get 23% of the profit per month on an investment of $15 million—it was our first high liquidity account. Our share of the profits is the equivalent of our putting $3.4 million of our own money at risk, except that our risk is reduced to zero, giving us the upside on $3.4 million and no downside. This is an example of AL achieved through promotional ability. In describing the types of good AL, I will provide an example of each using such names as Hunt, Pritzker, and Trump. In citing examples of both good and bad AL outside of MIMC, I'll tell the tale of good and bad AL in the same family: how forgetting a father's lessons cost two brothers a billion dollars.

MIMC is not the only organization that practices good AL. For example, Kohlberg, Kravis and Roberts (KKR), masters of LBO technique, have in 12 years assembled a group of companies whose gross sales almost equal those of GE, a company that took 60 years to build. Probably, KKR's general partners earned more money than GE's current superb management and have a net worth larger than most of GE's founding families, for that matter.

EXAMPLES

A. Financial
(When they think you have the money, somebody else will pick up the check.)

The raw power of AL, applied financially, is best demonstrated by Meshulam Riklis, an Israeli immigrant who began with the proverbial "nothing" and today controls a $3 billion empire. He created his empire through the effective use, or nonuse, of cash, coupled with excellent operating and financial management. If the use of cash was deemed necessary in an acquisition, Riklis projected the immediate generation of equivalent cash from the acquired company. Put another way, Riklis would not pay cash for a company that could not generate at least a similar amount of cash for his next move. Unless his conditions prevailed, he would not pursue the deal. However, it was always made known to the seller that Riklis's company, Rapid American, had the cash available to pay. In place of cash, he sold debt, issued warrants, sold divisions, and issued more stock. As an example, McCrory Corp. (owned fully by Rapid American) bought H. L. Green, based on the sale of Green's Canadian division for cash, which was in turn regenerated into McCrory for the cash in the tender offer for H. L. Green's stock. In Riklis's recent maneuver with EII, he has taken the company private and kept the debt public. Thus even though Riklis will not go down in history as a great retailing innovator, like for instance Ray Kroc of McDonald's, he will be remembered for managing his cash very well. He knows where every dollar is in his companies at any point in time. Total cash flow control, combined with his policy of buying companies with their own money, has made him sole equity holder of $3.0 billion worth of prime American corporate assets.

On the other hand, Robert Holmes á Court had no real cash flow control of the assets he owned. Holmes á Court began assembling his empire by making a series of tender offers to exchange shares in his then small company, Bell Resources, for shares in Broken Hill, Australia's largest company. He repeated this until he became Broken Hill's largest shareholder. Broken Hill's stock soared in the Australian bull-market rally, which enabled Holmes á Court to borrow money to buy shares in other companies such as Texaco and Sears PLC, which in turn served as collateral for further acquisitions. What Holmes á Court failed to do was to gain controlling interest in any of his holdings. Therefore, when the market crashed, he had no way of tapping their cash flow. He was merely another passive investor. Thus he was left with a tremendous amount of debt to service and no income to cover it. His downside risk was wide open, and his AL position was poor. In point of fact he had a reverse AL position; high risk and low possibility of return, the antithesis of Riklis's strategy.

B. Structural
(Every system has a bias: Every bias is a gift for someone.)

An excellent example of structural AL can be seen in a study that was conducted in 1978 by Theresa Havel on the risk inherent in owning government securities of varying maturities. Havel found that five-year Treasury notes provided 95% of the return of a 30-year T-bond. However, the five-year notes carried only 25%–30% of the price risk of the long bonds. In other words, the shorter maturity securities generated nearly the same return, but with substantially less risk than the longer maturity securities, thereby creating a stronger AL position. More recently, the Shearson Lehman bond indices have borne out the validity of Havel's findings, showing that long-term bonds returned 8.62% a year from January 1, 1973, to March 31, 1988, while 91-day T-bills returned 8.46%. The important point being that the slightly higher interest rate on the bonds carried with it 12 times the price risk of the T-bills as measured by the standard deviation of the price. In fact, from 1979 to 1982, the yield on five-year Treasury notes slightly surpassed that of the 30-year Treasury bonds. This is shown in the chart on the following page taken from Havel's company, Neuberger Berman. What Havel has shown is that, by minutely examining the inherent structure of a market, one can achieve good AL.

C. Entrepreneurial
(When two and two make forty.)

While Donald Trump was enmeshed in building the NYC Grand Hyatt, he heard over his car radio that there was a strike at the Hilton Hotel in Las Vegas, and that the stock had dropped sharply. That struck him as odd. After all, Hilton had 100 hotels—why did a strike in that one drive the stock down? He went to his office and looked at the 10-K for the Hilton Hotel (SEC full-disclosure report on file, yearly, for every public company). He found that 40% of the Hilton earnings came from the Las Vegas hotel, and that only 1% of earnings came from the NY Hilton. He would have been happy if the Grand Hyatt he was building did as well as the NY Hilton. However, he realized that casinos are a much better game at about the same risk.

To a builder like Trump, building casinos or hotel casinos is roughly the same task, except a casino has 40 times more payout, that is, better AL. Trump's father had built thousands of lower-middle-income buildings, and it is a game where when one and one make two, you make money. When one and one make one and three-quarters, you just break even. The difference between the first Trump fortune and the second is that Donald took his skills to a much higher profit-margin business and added a touch of show business to justify the higher price.

D. Operational
(Turning AL into a procedure.)

This type of AL shows up clearly in the business activities of the Pritzker family of Chicago. The Pritzkers own Hyatt Corp., Braniff, and a huge collection of industrial companies known as the Marmon Group, whose net worth is approximately 3.5 billion. Marmon got its start with the Pritzker's 1958 acquisition of Colson Caster Company, a failing Ohio maker of bicycles, wheelchair casters, and small navy rockets. This acquisition showed good AL because several appraisals showed the company could be liquidated for more than the purchase price, which essentially reduced the Pritzkers' risk to zero. Further, the purchase price had been pegged to asset value. Thus since Colson was sold for less than book value, US tax law at the time enabled Pritzker to receive a tax refund, which in turn reduced the assets further, leading to yet another refund. The Pritzkers thereby created a loss equivalent to all of the taxes the company had paid in the previous seven years, and so were able to lower the acquisition cost and turn a large part of the remainder of their purchase price into a working capital bridge loan until they received the tax money from the government. Hence, the Pritzkers began with good AL because they could liquidate for more than they paid and thus achieve zero risk. They then proceeded to improve their AL by taking advantage of the structure of the US tax law.

Although most of this paper deals with the financial side of AL, it should be noted that there's more to businesses than just numbers. They furnish actual goods and services to real people. For instance, the inventory of Colson Caster included 800 rejected and defective naval rockets. Upon the Pritzkers' acquisition of the company, these rockets were remachined and sold to the navy. A backward cost accounting system was redesigned, and in six months, the company's operations were profitable. A prime example of operational AL.

It is interesting to note that the operating styles of the Pritzkers, Hanson Trust, and Berkshire Hathaway (Warren Buffett's company) are all the same. Each operating unit employs a flat management style with all operating decisions handled at the unit level. All financial decisions and budgets, however, are vertical and must be approved from the top. In other words, the finances are the owners' business, and getting the product out is the operation managers' business. Profit sharing is determined on a unit basis rather than on a company basis. Therefore, if the company's earnings decrease while a particular unit's earnings rise, the unit manager will still receive his bonus. Strict financial control is at the very heart of AL. Without financial control, AL cannot be achieved, or maintained, for any length of time.

A final example of operational AL can be seen when we contrast the activities of Ray Hunt with those of his stepbrothers, Bunker and Lamar. Ray is the owner of

Hunt Oil Co., which when combined with his real estate investments, gives him a total net worth of well over one billion. Ray, unlike his stepbrothers, has followed his father's philosophy in his business.

The legendary H. L. Hunt won his first major oil holding, the basis of the family fortune, not in the oil fields, but across a poker table. In fact, in the beginning of his career, H. L. made more from poker than he did from drilling. His poker approach was the basis for his business approach in that he only bet where he could double his money in a year, and he made many bets so as to allow the law of large numbers to work in his favor. He once said that in his wild-catting days it never bothered him when he drilled a dry hole, because that meant that he was one step closer to drilling a winner. Additionally, he never bet so much on any one thing that the loss could stop him from letting the averages work for him, which is the way we operate at Mint.

This same philosophy can be seen in Ray Hunt's 1984 acquisition of his North Yemen field. The development of the field would have involved a major outlay, and given the country's risk, Ray sold 49% of his interests to Exxon, who agreed to pick up the full development costs of the field, making his share of the oil production nearly all profit and without risk.

Ray's stepbrothers, on the other hand, placed all their eggs in one basket—in one, highly leveraged, bet on silver. After they had cornered the market, there was no one left to whom they could sell. At that point, instead of cutting their losses, they pledged their income-producing assets to buy time for their losing silver trade. Their risk was asymmetrically against them rather than for them. They were in a position to lose far more than they could gain. Like his father, Ray risked a small percentage of his assets yearly for exploration. That year, North Yemen was one of his bets. Additionally, by taking on Exxon as a partner, he traded future earnings for a good AL position.

AL IN THEORY AND PRACTICE

MIMC is a good example of the theory and practice of AL.

The Man acquisition is an example of good AL for both sides. Man was worth over $100 million at the time and its risk was only $750,000, a small percentage of Man's net worth. They had the opportunity to buy 50% of Mint at a less than 5% chance of losing their $750,000, which set their real risk at $40,000, with a large body of statistical evidence showing them they could not lose.

From the HMO side we received the best AL factors possible; time and money. We got 5 years and the use of several million dollars for our own account plus an absolute income floor.

The structural factors that supported the initial partnership were:

a. predetermined probabilities in trading risk; and

b. the fact that futures margins paid T-bill rates and Man was able to borrow under prime, making financing cheap

These are the same factors that make our guarantee deals work. They allowed us to risk $250,000 out of a cash flow of $2 million at the time we launched the first guaranteed fund, which will earn us over $50 million by the end of this year. This will give us a return of 40 times our original investment of $250,000, which was 12.5% of our then cash flow.

We currently have accounts with the Man Group similar to Chardant. The oldest of these is the SAT account, which has earned more than 100% per year for 4 years. In achieving this record, the worst drawdown has been 16%. Almost no stocks have not dropped 16% at least once during the same 4-year period, but virtually none have appreciated 100% per year on average.

The reasons the Chardant type of account has done so well are:

a. low transaction costs, which enable us to adjust risk frequently and a Run D system, which acts as an internal hedge in sharp reversal situations, and that

b. all "bets" are kept equal at risk in size to prevent the risks from becoming disproportionate

All of these factors combine to control the risk, yet allow the full benefits of increased leverage, making the risk asymmetrical to the leverage.

AL CULTURE

To make AL work, you need three main ingredients: time, knowledge, and money.

a. Time—normally the faster you have to move, the riskier the move; but with time to pick spots, you can move with virtually no risk.

b. Knowledge—you can't know the odds until you know the game. If you don't know the odds, you can't make an intelligent bet. A good example of the advantage of clearly defining the game is MIMC trading. At MIMC, we know nothing about the underlying assets of the futures, and we know everything about how to trade them. If we had used leverage without that knowledge, it would have led to either immediate or eventual disaster.

c. Money—buys you time, buys you knowledge, and allows the long-term odds to work in your favor.

Jay Pritzker never overreaches if a deal is too big for him. He either gets a partner or he passes. In other words, he never gets out of good AL position. His comment on the acquisition of Braniff sums it up beautifully: "Braniff will cost me 50 million dollars. If it works, it's worth 500 million; if it doesn't, I can live with the loss."

PROPOSED AL PROJECT

We have identified, via our relationship with Dick Elden, a number of money managers with returns in the 15%–20% range with very little volatility and no losing quarters. The performance of each manager is not correlated with any of the others and with the general market, because they are using, essentially, market techniques.

Despite the higher quality of the actual track record, let's assume that the worst-case drawdown risk is 20%. Additionally, assume that we treat this activity like another line of business within the Man Group and provide it with capital of, say, $5,000,000 and a line of credit of, say, $20mm. Basis a gross return of 20%, this activity would produce $5mm before interest expense of $2mm, for a net return of $3mm or 60% on risk capital. At a gross return of 15%, the return on risk capital is 35%.

Given that this stable of managers has in fact shown no losing quarters over a protracted period, the risk adjusted returns from this business are even better. For example, if we assume that the real risk is 10% of capital instead of the 20% above, then the net returns increase to 120% basis 20% gross return and 87.5% basis 15% gross.

This business is clearly a leveraged arbitrage between cost of money and the results of the portfolio of managers. As noted elsewhere, leverage applied without knowledge leads to either immediate or eventual disaster. What makes this proposition a strong candidate for an initial AL project is that the track record of the managers in the portfolio is subject to quantitative analysis as is MIMC's trading. We can take our methodology of risk measurement and management and "leverage" it again with respect to these managers, given a long enough track record. Two other practical requirements emerge from this analysis:

   a. the need to make a long-term commitment to this
      business so the long-term odds can work; and
   b. cost of money should be locked in, given that these
      returns do not tend to rise with interest rates.

Overall, as a business, this activity compares very favorably with that of the Man Group's commodity trading activities when evaluated on a risk/reward basis. For example, Man's sugar trading activities seek to produce a return of 40% of risk capital while tolerating a risk of 36% of capital in terms of position size—roughly one for one. The business outlined above produces equivalent risk/reward, without adding the additional risk dimensions of credit and counterparty default.

AL WORKING GROUPS

We should set up an AL Group based in New York and reporting to LH/HMcG. This group would be tasked with finding AL opportunities in the corporate sector. The strategy would involve buying control of a public vehicle for a dollar consideration in the $2.5–$5mm range and subsequently raising additional capital against this business and balance sheet. Given our strengths—money management and financial products—this first step is likely to be in this area, and it is thought that beyond this vehicle the group would focus (but not exclusively) on the insurance and S&L sectors for the next target. Robert Rosenkrantz nicely illustrates the opportunities. In 1987, with $20mm in capital and $240mm borrowed from GE Credit, he took control of Reliance Insurance Company and $800mm of assets. With Dick Elden's advice, he introduced a portfolio strategy based on a diversified mixed asset and method approach. He then proceeded to double the net earnings in the first year.

Staffing of the AL Group would consist initially of two people, with education and experience to enable them to work independently within a framework provided. The cost of this operation would be in the area of $200mm for the first year.

I would like to state, for the record, that the concept described here is my own, and the responsibility for material rests solely with me.

I would also like to thank Harvey McGrath and Patrick Dumas for helping to shape my ideas into a coherent presentation, and Peter Matthews and Michael Delman, without whom there would be no working model of AL. Also, I would like to share the blame with David Federman, who, over dinner, asked if I would write down my ideas on AL and its applications to running a business.

L. Hite

—INDEX—

— ABOUT THE AUTHOR —

Larry Hite has over 35 years of experience as a successful trader and investor and is one of Wall Street's revered moneymakers. In 1972 he published the seminal paper "Game Theory Applications" in which he suggested game theory could be used in trading futures and he went on to put his theories into practice. He cofounded Mint Investment Management and led the firm to creating one of the industry's first systematic trend following CTAs with its famous Statistical Approach to trading. He structured a groundbreaking joint venture between Mint and Man Group to create and distribute alternative investment products.

Larry created the first principal guarantee fund, Mint Guaranteed Investment Fund, and the success of this product led to his involvement in over 50 subsequent guaranteed product structures. Mint went on to be the first CTA to manage over $1 billion in assets. His success earned him industrywide recognition and he was featured in Jack Schwager's bestselling book *Market Wizards*.

In 2001 Larry created a family office called Hite Capital Management where he directs his own investments and continues his research into the field of systematic trading.